Management for Professionals

The Springer series *Management for Professionals* comprises high-level business and management books for executives. The authors are experienced business professionals and renowned professors who combine scientific background, best practice, and entrepreneurial vision to provide powerful insights into how to achieve business excellence.

More information about this series at http://www.springer.com/series/10101

Steven De Haes · Laura Caluwe ·
Tim Huygh · Anant Joshi

Governing Digital Transformation

Guidance for Corporate Board Members

 Springer

Steven De Haes
Antwerp, Belgium

Tim Huygh
Antwerp, Belgium

Laura Caluwe
Antwerp, Belgium

Anant Joshi
Maastricht, The Netherlands

ISSN 2192-8096   ISSN 2192-810X   (electronic)
Management for Professionals
ISBN 978-3-030-30269-6   ISBN 978-3-030-30267-2   (eBook)
https://doi.org/10.1007/978-3-030-30267-2

This Springer imprint is published by the registered company Springer Nature Switzerland AG
The registered company address is: Gewerbestrasse 11, 6330 Cham, Switzerland

Preface

Boards of directors are ultimately accountable for strategic decision-making and control in organizations. Financial and legal matters sometimes dominate the agendas of board meetings, which is often reflected in board composition. But what about IT-related matters? This is a prominent question in an era, where IT is a crucial contributing factor to the competitiveness of many organizations.

In our research, we have observed that board members often recognize the need for more board-level engagement in digital strategy and oversight, to make sure that their organization can foster the full potential of digital transformation. However, we have also found that many board members are seeking guidance and advise on how to realize this type of board-level engagement. This research is part of an extensive research program installed by the University of Antwerp—Antwerp Management School, CEGEKA, KPMG Belgium and Samsung Belgium on the role of the board in IT governance. The premise of this research program is that boards need to extend their governance accountability, from often a mono-focus on finance and legal as a proxy to corporate governance, to include technology and provide digital leadership and organizational capabilities to ensure that the enterprise's IT sustains and extends the enterprise's strategies and objectives. With this book, we provide guidance for board members on how to execute their IT-related duties and demonstrate the importance of board involvement in IT governance.

Our goal was to create clear and readily applicable guidance for board members to govern digital transformation. At the same time, we balanced rigor and relevance. That is, the results are based on academic research that was executed by a research group with many years of experience in the research domain of IT governance.

The book contains three main parts. The first part provides a roadmap for board members towards digital transformation. Our goal is to provide clear and applicable guidance for boards of directors on how to shape their involvement in governing digital assets. The importance of such involvement is demonstrated in the second part of the book. The third part provides unique insights into the inner workings of a specific board of directors, with a focus on its IT governance structures and processes. We describe how this board tackles today's digital challenges and illustrate the importance of adapting IT governance mechanisms to the specific context of the organization in general, and to the board in specific.

We hope that with this book we will inspire board members to tackle the challenges of the digital age and that we can contribute to further developing the emerging knowledge domain of board-level IT governance.

Antwerp, Belgium   Steven De Haes
Antwerp, Belgium   Laura Caluwe
Antwerp, Belgium   Tim Huygh
Maastricht, The Netherlands   Anant Joshi

Acknowledgements

We would like to thank all involved in our research. Without the support of these people, we would not have been able to develop this book.

We would like to express our gratitude toward all practitioners who shared their insights on the topic of board-level IT governance. More specifically, we would like to thank the board members that were part of the focus groups and interviews that were organized in the context of this research. Furthermore, we gratefully acknowledge the business and IT managers from the University of Antwerp, who allowed us to develop the case study on board-level IT governance at the university.

We appreciate the support provided for this project by the Faculty of Business and Economics of the University of Antwerp and the Antwerp Management School. We would also like to thank everyone involved from our partners CEGEKA, KPMG Belgium and Samsung Belgium, for enabling us to balance rigor and relevance, providing access to practitioners and contributing in many other ways to this research.

Contents

1   **Introduction: The Board in the Digital Age**   1
     1.1   What Is Board-level IT Governance?   2

2   **A Roadmap Towards Governing Digital Transformation**   5
     2.1   Task 1: Install—A Three-Step Approach   5
         2.1.1   Step 1: Articulate an Understanding of the Role
                of IT in the Organization   6
         2.1.2   Step 2: Establish the Appropriate Governance
                Structures   7
         2.1.3   Step 3: Give Direction and Provide Oversight
                by Asking Critical Questions   10
     2.2   Task 2: Measure—A Board-level Dashboard for Digital Strategy
         and Oversight   11
     2.3   Task 3: Report—IT Governance Disclosure   17
         2.3.1   Why Boards Should Report on IT Governance   17
         2.3.2   The State of Practice in Belgium   18
         2.3.3   A Call for Action for Governing Boards   22
     2.4   Conclusion   22

3   **Why Should Boards Care?**   25
     3.1   The Benefits of Board IT Governance   25
     3.2   How Does IT Fit into the Board's Duties?   26
         3.2.1   Provide Oversight on IT-Related Matters
                (Agency Theory)   27
         3.2.2   Provide Guidance and Direction on IT-Related Matters
                (Stewardship Theory)   27
         3.2.3   Build Unique Digital Capabilities for Competitiveness
                (Resource Dependence Theory and Resource-Based
                View of the Firm)   27
     3.3   Conclusion   28

4   Learning from Peers 29
   4.1   The Case of the University of Antwerp 29
   4.2   Why Did the University of Antwerp Initiate Board-Level
       Involvement in Digital Strategy and Oversight? 30
   4.3   How Did the University of Antwerp Initiate More Board-Level
       Involvement in Digital Strategy and Oversight? 31
       4.3.1   Guiding Principles 31
       4.3.2   Governing Structures 31
       4.3.3   Governing Processes 34
   4.4   Realizing the Value of Board-level IT Governance 37
       4.4.1   Task 1: Install 38
       4.4.2   Task 2: Measure 40
   4.5   Key Takeaways 44

5   Governance Objectives to Lead Digital Transformation 47
   5.1   COBIT 2019 47
   5.2   Ensured Governance Framework Setting and Maintenance
       (EDM01) 48
   5.3   Ensured Benefits Delivery (EDM02) 50
   5.4   Ensured Risk Optimization (EDM03) 52
   5.5   Ensured Resource Optimization (EDM04) 53
   5.6   Ensured Stakeholder Engagement (EDM05) 57
   5.7   Conclusion 60

References 63

Chapter 1
Introduction: The Board in the Digital Age

> "Board IT Governance is related to the fundamental mission of the board, which is strategy and oversight. Given the nature of IT, I believe the board should adopt an integrated approach with regard to IT issues, because at the end of the day, these IT matters affect every element, every component of the business."
> —Non-executive board member

Boards of directors are ultimately accountable for strategic decision-making and control in organizations [1]. Financial and legal matters sometimes dominate the agendas of board meetings, which is often reflected in board composition [2]. But what about IT-related matters? This is a prominent question in an era where IT is a crucial contributing factor to the competitiveness of many organizations.

Indeed, organizations are increasingly dependent on IT for the creation of business value [3, 4]. Digital disruption is all around us, and a vast number of organizations around the globe is actively thinking about digital transformation [2]. Yet empirical evidence seems to indicate that boards of directors are not as involved in IT-related strategic decision-making and control as they should be [3, 5, 6]. Emerging research calls for more board-level engagement in IT governance and identifies serious consequences for digitized organizations in case the board is not involved in setting direction towards and being in control of the digital assets. The collapse of Eastman Kodak for example was primarily induced by their inability to keep up with technology change [4]. In terms of the role of the board to provide direction for the organization, digital assets have become fundamental for managing enterprise resources and business processes, dealing with suppliers and customers, and enabling increasingly global transactions [3]. Disruptive technologies can impact complete business and income models, or even make sectors obsolete in short timeframes (e.g. AirBnB, Uber) [4]. But also, in terms of accountability towards control, there is a growing need to comply with an increasing amount of regulatory and legal requirements of which many also impact IT (e.g. privacy) [7, 8]. Furthermore, the continuity of reliability of most primary and secondary

© Springer Nature Switzerland AG 2020
S. De Haes et al., *Governing Digital Transformation*, Management for Professionals,
https://doi.org/10.1007/978-3-030-30267-2_1

business processes relies heavily on IT [9]. Finally, there is a rising need for boards of directors to provide transparency on how digitals assets are governed in their organization. Voluntary disclosure theory predicts that digitized firms can improve their liquidity and firm valuation through better information provisioning on the way they govern IT [10, 11].

Additionally, empirical evidence shows that board-level IT governance enables better organizational performance while managing the business risks of the organization. Research shows that high levels of board-level IT governance, regardless of existing IT needs, will improve organizational performance [12]. Companies with a comprehensive digital leadership function, both in terms of performance (+9%) and profitability (+23%) and in terms of a greater market valuation (+12%) show superior financial performance [2]. Regarding risk drivers, there is a need to comply with an increasing amount of regulatory and legal requirements of which many also impact IT. As such, these regulatory requirements redefine director responsibilities for IT governance [13]. Although business risk resulting from IT has traditionally been a focus area solely for IT professionals, this is not the case anymore [10, 13, 14].

Notwithstanding both the empirically and theoretically demonstrated importance of board-level IT governance, other studies point out that on average the involvement of boards in IT governance is low, less than 20% of the boards are taking up accountability for governing their digital assets, and that boards should become more IT savvy to be able to govern the digitized organization. Or in other words, boards need to extend their governance accountability, including technology and provide digital leadership and organizational capabilities to ensure that the enterprise's IT sustains and extends the enterprise's strategies and objectives [2, 3, 5, 6].

Despite the agreement between researchers and practitioners on the need for board involvement in IT governance, it appears that this is more the exception than the rule in practice [3, 5, 6]. In our research, we have observed that, indeed, board members often recognize the need for more board engagement in digital strategy and oversight. At the same time, many of them are seeking advise on how to realize this type of engagement. With this book, we provide guidance for board members on how to execute their IT-related duties.

1.1   What Is Board-level IT Governance?

IT governance, otherwise referred to as "enterprise governance of IT" or "corporate governance of IT", is a focus area of corporate governance that is concerned with the organization's IT assets. In analogy to corporate governance, it is concerned with the oversight of IT assets, their contribution to business value and the mitigation of IT-related risks [15]. A common referenced definition comes from De Haes and Van Grembergen [46] who state that:

Enterprise governance of IT is an integral part of corporate governance exercised by the board and addresses the definition and implementation of processes, structures and relational mechanisms in the organization that enable both business and IT people to execute their responsibilities in support of business/IT alignment and the creation of business value from IT-enabled business investments.

Essentially, the ultimate goal of governing IT is to enhance IT's delivery of business value and to mitigate IT risks. IT value delivery is driven by strategic alignment, which concerns the strategic fit of business and IT and the integration of organizational and IT infrastructure an processes [16]. Both IT value delivery and IT risk management require adequate allocation of resources and continuous performance measurement. As a consequence, many sources identify five areas or domains of attention in the context of IT governance that need to be addressed [17 −20]:

- Strategic alignment, with focus on aligning IT with the business and collaborative solutions
- Value delivery, concentrating on optimizing expenses and proving the value of IT
- Risk management, addressing the IT related business risks
- Resource management, optimizing IT related knowledge and resources
- Performance measurement, monitoring IT enabled investment and service delivery

In practice, IT governance can be implemented using a set of structures, processes, and relational mechanisms [15, 21, 22]. IT governance structures include organizational units and roles responsible for making IT decisions and for enabling contacts between business and IT management decision-making functions (e.g. IT steering committee). This can be seen as a kind of blueprint of how the governance framework will be structurally organized. IT governance processes refer to the formalization and institutionalization of strategic IT decision-making and IT monitoring procedures, to ensure that daily behaviors are consistent with policies and provide input back to decisions (e.g. portfolio management). Finally, IT governance relational mechanisms are about the active participation of, and collaborative relationship among, corporate executives, IT management, and business management and include job-rotation, announcements, advocates, channels and education efforts. Some examples of these structures, processes and relational mechanisms are provided in Fig. 1.1.

Fig. 1.1 Structures, processes and relational mechanisms for IT governance [46]

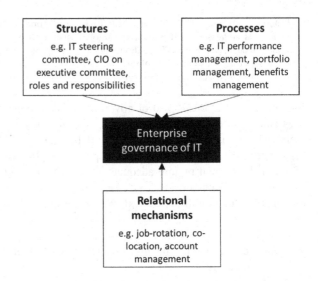

IT governance resides both at executive management-level and at the level of the board of directors [23]. Hence, board-level IT governance specifically addresses the role of the board in IT-related strategic decision-making and control.

Chapter 2
A Roadmap Towards Governing Digital Transformation

In order to take up accountability for governing digital assets and reap the associated benefits, we put forward three crucial board tasks: install, measure and report.

Task 1 "install" consists of designing the appropriate governing system for your organization and setting it in motion. We propose a three-step approach for boards to engage in digital strategy and oversight.

In order to adequately perform their IT oversight role, it is vital that boards measure the performance of the IT governance system that was established, hence task 2 "measure". We have created a board-level dashboard for digital strategy and oversight as a supporting tool for this performance measurement. This dashboard will help boards to evaluate whether their board-level IT governance approach is implemented properly, whether it is generating the desired outcomes and how it can be improved.

Investors might be willing to invest more in organizations with adequately controlled digital assets. We believe that as the dependency on IT will continue to grow within all industries, IT governance disclosure might well become a critical piece of the non-financial information in most annual reports. As such, boards will become increasingly incentivized to disclose on the matter, with them increasing their own expectations towards executive management. That is why we identified "report" as task 3.

2.1 Task 1: Install—A Three-Step Approach

Based on our research, we propose a three-step approach for boards to increase their engagement in IT governance (Fig. 2.1).

© Springer Nature Switzerland AG 2020
S. De Haes et al., *Governing Digital Transformation*, Management for Professionals,
https://doi.org/10.1007/978-3-030-30267-2_2

Fig. 2.1 The roadmap towards governing digital transformation

2.1.1 Step 1: Articulate an Understanding of the Role of IT in the Organization

> You have to do a good evaluation of your strategy and how crucial IT is in realizing your strategy.
>
> —Non-executive board member

As the required role of the board in IT governance might be different in diverse types of organizations, the first step the board should take is understanding and determining the significance of IT and its role with respect to the business. In this context, an instrumental toolkit is provided through the strategic impact grid of Nolan and McFarlan [24], which is shown in Fig. 2.2. Depending on the role of IT for the organization, the board-level IT governance approach will be different.

The strategic impact grids defines four "IT use modes" along two axes (contingencies). A low need for new information technology entails a defensive IT strategy, whereas a high need requires an offensive IT strategy. The latter implies that business processes, income models, etc. will or need to be innovated through technology to gain new markets and customers, to improve quality of services, etc.

Fig. 2.2 Strategic impact grid [26]

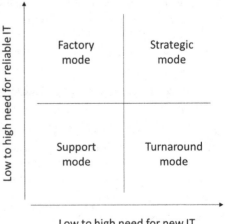

The spectrum is completed by the need for reliable information technology: within a defensive IT strategy, a high need for reliability results in a "factory" use mode, a low need results in a "support" use mode. Factory mode implies that many or most of the business processes will fail to work when technology fails, with immediate impact on business continuity, turnover, sales etc. Within an offensive strategy, a high need for reliability results in a "strategic" use mode, a low need results in a "turnaround" mode.

It is possible that the board will conclude that their activities reside in different quadrants as proposed in Fig. 2.2, or that their activities continuously switch between quadrants. For example, some of the key business processes might require mainly very reliable and cost-efficient support of IT (for example production processes in factory mode), while in parallel new products and services are developed that require innovative IT solutions (for example marketing processes in strategic mode). It is important for the board to understand and articulate such bi-modal or dynamic requirements in this step. Next, it is up to the board to ensure that the organizational capabilities are designed in such a way that these requirements are met.

2.1.2   Step 2: Establish the Appropriate Governance Structures

Introduce the right people with the right background in the board. Because if you have a big legal issue, you also introduce your lawyers on that. But make sure you have people who focus on it from a business perspective also, that is very important.

—Non-executive board member

Depending on the role of IT in the organization, an appropriate governance structure needs to be established. For organizations in the offensive mode, the board should consider including the IT-related topic as a fixed agenda item within the board's agenda or the agenda of the "strategy committee" supporting the board. Of course, this requires the chairman to take the necessary steps to make to board more "IT savvy" by appointing a member with IT governance expertise or evolving towards more multi-disciplined directors.

Alternatively, the board could consider establishing a separate IT Strategy and Oversight Committee at the same level as the board-level audit or strategy committee. The essential advantage of the advisory role of the IT Strategy and Oversight Committee is facilitating deliberations on technology in order to help make informed decisions. To set up an IT Strategy and Oversight Committee, the appropriate chairman and members need to be selected. Independent directors, with IT governance-related expertise, could be considered to be the members of the committee. A charter has to be made of which a draft generic layout is provided below. Of course, the selection of the appropriate committee where IT will be discussed or prepared for the board, and the related charter requirements, will

IT Strategy and Oversight Committee Charter

Name
IT Strategy and Oversight Committee

Purpose
To assist the board in giving direction and being in control on enterprise's IT-related matters.

Responsibility
The committee should ensure that IT is a regular item on the board's agenda and that it is addressed in a structured
manner. In addition, the committee must ensure that the board has the information it needs to make
informed decisions that are essential to achieve the ultimate objectives of IT governance. Those objectives are:
• Strategic alignment, with focus on aligning business and IT strategies
• Value delivery, concentrating on optimizing expenses and proving the value of IT
• Risk management, addressing the IT related business risks
• Resource management, optimising IT related knowledge and resources
• Performance management, monitoring IT enabled investment and service delivery

Authority
The IT Strategy and Oversight Committee operates at the board level but does not assume the board's
governance accountability nor make final decisions. Instead, it assists the board on
current and future IT-related issues.
The IT Strategy and Oversight Committee must work in partnership with the other board committees to
provide input to, review and amend the aligned corporate and IT strategies. Possible partnerships are with:
• The Audit Committee, on major IT risks
• The Business Strategy Committee, on value delivery and alignment
• The Compensation Committee, on performance measurement

Fig. 2.3 IT Strategy and Oversight Committee Charter [18]

Membership

The IT Strategy and Oversight Committee is composed of a chairman and several board members. The
members should be selected on the basis of their knowledge and expertise in understanding the business
impacts of information and related technology.
The success of the IT Strategy and Oversight Committee depends on an objective and business-oriented
understanding of the organization's IT issues. An effective mix of members who understand the business
operations and can challenge IT assumptions is likely to increase the IT Oversight success in achieving its
goals. For this reason, the committee should invite ex-officio permanent representation of key executives
and internal or external independent experts, while remaining mindful of confidentiality requirements.

Meetings

The IT Strategy and Oversight Committee should meet when needed and as often as needed to accomplish
its duties. The committee should report its findings and recommendations to the board. In addition, the
committee's meeting agenda, minutes and supporting documents should be provided to the board so that
board members not sitting on the committee may submit their comments to the committee chairman.

Fig. 2.3 (continued)

highly depend on the existing dynamics and operating principles of the board. A sample charter is shown in Fig. 2.3.

In case IT is of less strategic importance (defensive mode), the audit committee could at least take up the IT oversight role as part of its duties. Also, the risk committee and audit committee are seen as valid structures by which board-level IT governance can be increased, certainly in view of the board's limited time. However, the limited scope of these committees might result in an adequate focus on the risk aspect but insufficient attention towards the value and performance aspects of IT. Finally, the organization's bandwidth might not allow for installing separate committees within the board. In that case, it is up to the board's chairman to bring in IT governance expertise within the board's team or consider multi-skilled directors. Some audit committee recommendations are provided in Fig. 2.4.

Audit Committee Recommendations

Membership of the audit committee
- Consider the appointment of an independent board member within the audit committee who has expertise on IT governance related elements
- Consider regular invitation of the CIO to understand IT related risks

Implication towards internal & external audit
- Ensure that the internal or external audit function has sufficient knowledge and expertise around IT governance and management aspect (to assess risk and value of IT)

Agenda
- Ensure IT related risks are yearly addressed on the audit committee agenda

Fig. 2.4 Recommendations for the audit committee

2.1.3 Step 3: Give Direction and Provide Oversight by Asking Critical Questions

> Asking critical questions is a responsibility of every board member, regardless of whether he's a lawyer or a finance specialist or manager or what have you. You have to have sector knowledge, you have to understand what the heartbeat of the organization is, and you have to do your homework related to technological developments, what is going on in the world.
>
> —Non-executive board member

Once the IT governance accountability is established at board level, asking "the right" questions is an effective way to get started. Of course, those responsible for governance want good answers to these questions. Then they want action. Then they need follow-up. Here are some sample questions (Fig. 2.5), categorized according to the role of IT within the company. The more you move from the support mode towards strategic mode, the more questions you can leverage from the different quadrants.

In asking and answering these questions, a climate of openness and transparency should exist between the board and executive management on IT-related topics, in both directions and in a language that all stakeholders can understand. This implies a pivotal role for the CIO, in providing support to the board on IT-related topics and taking their advice towards further (digital) strategy.

Fig. 2.5 Asking "the right" questions linked to the IT strategic impact grid [24]

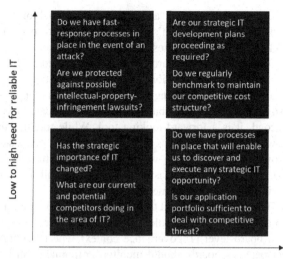

Low to high need for new IT

2.2   Task 2: Measure—A Board-level Dashboard for Digital Strategy and Oversight

In order to adequately perform their IT oversight role, it is vital that boards measure the performance of the IT governance system that was established. Indeed, the Economic Co-operation and Development (OECD) principles of corporate governance[1] state that one of the key functions of the board is *"monitoring the effectiveness of the company's governance practices and making changes as needed"*. As IT governance is an integral part of corporate governance, this principle applies to IT governance as well. That is why we have created a board-level dashboard for digital strategy and oversight. This dashboard will help boards to evaluate whether their board-level IT governance approach is implemented properly, whether it is generating the desired outcomes and how it can be improved.

The structure of the board-level dashboard for digital strategy and oversight is based on the balanced scorecard. The balanced scorecard is a widely used tool for performance measurement. It was introduced by Kaplan and Norton [25] to encourage organizations to not only use financial indicators to keep track of performance. They argue that financial indicators do not necessarily measure how well an organization is executing its strategy. Instead, in addition to financial indicators, organizations need to add measures relating to customer satisfaction, internal

---

[1]The Organization for Economic Co-operation and Development (OECD) principles on corporate governance are an international benchmark for corporate governance, which many countries have used as a basis for their corporate governance codes.

processes and learning and growth. The goal of the balanced scorecard is to translate an organization's strategy into a set of performance measures concerning each of these perspectives.

The balanced scorecard offers some unique benefits. First, it entails a top-down approach. An organization first needs to crystalize its strategy and derive appropriate measures accordingly, whereas traditional approaches tend to be bottom-up, establishing measures that originate from local activities and ad hoc processes. Second, it is a forward-looking tool. While traditional financial indicators tell us how the organization has been performing in the past, the other perspectives will provide information on where to go in the future. Third, it mixes internal and external perspectives. Lastly, the scorecard will help organization leaders to focus on the most important measures.

To create a dashboard that boards can use to monitor their effectiveness in taking up a digital leadership role, the concepts of the balanced scorecard were translated to a board-level IT governance context. The resulting dashboard consists of four perspectives boards should monitor: corporate contribution, stakeholders' orientation, internal practices and future orientation. A mission and more specific objectives are identified for each perspective, indicating the desired outcomes. To monitor the realization of these objectives, metrics are added. An overview of these elements is shown in Fig. 2.6.

Fig. 2.6 Board-level dashboard for digital strategy and oversight

Board level dashboard for digital strategy and oversight

	Mission	Objectives
Corporate contribution	Ensuring maximum value through IT with reasonable risk	Strategic alignment
		Value delivery
		Risk management
Stakeholders' orientation	Measuring up to stakeholders' expectations	Legal and ethical compliance
		Transparency
Internal practices	Ensuring effective and sustained IT governance	Structures
		Processes
Future orientation	Building foundations for IT governance delivery	Skills and knowledge
		Culture

What boards can expect as outcome from their digital oversight and strategy

What boards should do to ensure digital oversight and strategy

Mission	Objectives	Board metrics	Actual Value	Target Value	Support	Factory	Turnaround	Strategic
Future orientation — Building foundations for IT governance delivery	Skills and knowledge	Percentage of board members with expertise related to mangement or governance of IT				x	x	x
	Culture	Level of awareness of IT strategic importance among board members / organization's dependence on IT			x	x	x	x
		Level of awareness of the board's role in IT governance			x	x	x	x
		Number of board directives that discuss the role of IT in the organzation				x	x	x

Fig. 2.7 Board-level dashboard for digital strategy and oversight—Future orientation

IT governance can be deployed using a holistic set of structures, processes and relational mechanisms. The starting point of future proof board-level IT governance resides in the skills and culture, which can be categorized as relational mechanisms. These foundations are presented in the **"future orientation"** perspective (Fig. 2.7). Hence, the future orientation mission is *"Building foundations for IT governance delivery"*. Research indicates that an inhibitor of board-level IT governance is the perception that IT governance is not a topic that should be discussed by the board [9, 17]. That is why a first step towards board-level IT governance is the creation of a culture that acknowledges the importance of IT and willingness by the board to become involved in IT governance. Furthermore, when business and IT professionals do not understand each other, business/IT alignment will never be fully attained. Hence, a board with correct skills and knowledge is essential [9, 12, 23].

Key IT governance structures and processes at board level are identified in the **"internal practices"** perspective (Fig. 2.8). The goal is to *"ensure effective and sustained IT governance"*. A structure put forward by many authors is an IT strategy and oversight committee at board level [12, 19, 26]. Such a committee can support the board in taking up their digital leadership role. The suggested processes relate to the frequency and type of IT discussions held by the board [12, 23, 27].

It is important to evaluate the IT governance system from the perspective of all relevant stakeholders, including the board of directors, executive management, business and IT users but also customers, shareholders and regulators. Therefore, the mission of the **"stakeholders' orientation"** perspective (Fig. 2.9) is *"Measuring up*

Mission	Objectives	Board metrics	Value		IT use mode			
			Actual Value	Target Value	Support	Factory	Turnaround	Strategic
Internal practices / Ensuring effective and sustained IT governance	Structures	Number of meetings of IT strategy and oversight committee					x	x
		Level of attendance of board members to IT strategy and oversight committee					x	x
	Processes	Number of times IT is an item on the audit committee agenda	x	x				
		Percentage of time spent on IT risk topics during board meetings				x		x
		Percentage of time spent on IT innovation topics during board meetings					x	x
		Number of times IT risk topics are items on the board meeting agenda				x		x
		Number of times IT innovation topics are items on the board meeting agenda					x	x
		Frequency of suggestions/decisions/advise by the board on IT				x	x	x
		Number of presentations from the CIO to the board				x	x	x

Fig. 2.8 Board-level dashboard for digital strategy and oversight—Internal practices

to stakeholders' expectations". As one of the board's most important stakeholders are regulators, legal and ethical compliance should be monitored closely [28]. Furthermore, stakeholders should be informed about IT governance by the board. As research indicates that board-level IT governance leads to increased organizational performance and theories such as voluntary disclosure theory and agency theory predict that firms can improve their liquidity and firm valuation through better information intermediation, we argue that organizations can benefit from IT governance disclosure [29].

The ultimate goal of IT governance is business value through the alignment of business and IT. That is why we can translate the financial perspective of the original balanced scorecard into a **"corporate contribution"** perspective

Stakeholders' orientation	Measuring up to stakeholders' expectations	Legal and ethical compliance	Board metrics	Value		IT use mode			
				Actual Value	Target Value	Support	Factory	Turnaround	Strategic
		Legal and ethical compliance	Cost of IT non-compliance, including settlements and fines, and the impact of reputational loss					X	X
			Number of regulatory non-compliance issues causing public comment or negative publicity					X	X
		Transparency	Level of disclosure on IT governance in annual reports				X	X	X

Fig. 2.9 Board-level dashboard for digital strategy and oversight—Stakeholders' orientation

(Fig. 2.10) in the board-level IT governance balanced scorecard. The mission defined for this perspective is *"Ensuring maximum profit through IT with reasonable risk"*. This entails three primary objectives: strategic alignment, value delivery and risk management.

For each objective, several metrics were identified. Simply specifying each metric's actual value will not help boards to better execute their digital oversight role. Boards should identify a target value for each metric that is monitored. Doing so will give meaning to the actual values and enable boards to evaluate their performance.

It is important to note that the scorecard perspectives are interlinked. Causal relationships between them can be identified (Fig. 2.11). For example, board members with appropriate IT expertise (future orientation) may have more IT discussions (internal practices), which in turn will increase legal compliance (stakeholders' orientation) and will ultimately lead to reduced IT risk (corporate contribution). In other words, the future orientation and internal practices perspectives refer to **what boards need to do** to ensure digital oversight and strategy. Accordingly, the metrics belonging to these perspectives can be called "lead indicators". Contrarily, the corporate contribution and stakeholders' orientation perspectives illustrate the **outcomes boards can expect** from their digital oversight and strategy. Hence, metrics within these perspectives can be called "lag indicators".

A first step in implementing IT governance at board level is articulating an understanding of the role of IT in the organization. This is a crucial step, as the best way for boards to take up their digital leadership role is not the same for every type of organization.

Mission	Objectives	Board metrics	Value		IT use mode			
			Actual Value	Target Value	Support	Factory	Turnaround	Strategic
Corporate contribution — Ensuring maximum value through IT with reasonable risk	Strategic alignment	Level of alignment of business strategy with the distribution in the IT budget between IT investments and operations			x	x	x	x
		Percentage of IT development capacity engaged in strategic projects					x	x
		Fit between business strategy and IT strategy			x	x	x	x
	Value delivery	Percent of IT-enabled investments where claimed benefits are met or exceeded			x	x	x	x
	Risk management	Number of security incidents causing financial loss, business disruption or public embarrassment				x		x
		Number of business processing hours lost due to unplanned service interruptions				x		x
		Number of unresolved high risk audit recommendations				x		x

Fig. 2.10 Board-level dashboard for digital strategy and oversight—Corporate contribution

Fig. 2.11 Causal relationships between scorecard perspectives

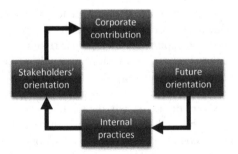

The different IT use modes as introduced in *Task 1—Step 1: Articulate an understanding of the role of IT in the organization* call for different board-level IT governance approaches. For example, boards of organizations in factory mode need to actively monitor the security of IT. However, for boards operating in an organization in support mode, IT security is not a priority. The same principle applies for the way in which boards evaluate their IT governance effectiveness. Certain metrics are more important to monitor than others for each IT use mode. The last column in the dashboard illustrates this principle: important metrics for each IT use mode are marked with an "x". For example, boards should monitor "*the number of security incidents causing financial loss, business disruption or public embarrassment*" in factory and strategic mode, as the need for reliable IT is high. However, the need for reliable IT is low in support and turnaround mode. Therefore, this metric is of less importance to boards in these modes.

The dashboard is meant to be used as a tool that boards can customize to meet their specific needs. Not only can custom objectives and metrics be added, but the dashboard can also be extended with additional information to facilitate board members even more in taking up their digital oversight role. Examples of additional information are: the priority of each objective or metric, benchmarks for each metric, actions that could be taken to improve actual values, etc.

2.3 Task 3: Report—IT Governance Disclosure

As organizations increasingly rely on digital assets to create business value, one might expect that investors are interested in how these assets are governed. As a consequence, we believe that IT governance disclosure might well become a critical piece of the non-financial information in most annual reports. Hence, we identified "report" as task 3.

2.3.1 Why Boards Should Report on IT Governance

In their empirical study, Higgs et al. [30] analyzed the link between board level technology committees and reported security breaches. They found that the negative market reaction to reported security breaches is mitigated by the presence of a technology committee. This suggests that the presence of such a committee is positively perceived by the market. More generally, research shows that "high levels of board-level IT governance, regardless of existing IT needs, increased organizational performance" [12], clearly demonstrating the importance of board taking up their accountability related to IT. Researchers concluded that boards should not shy away from governing and controlling the IT assets for their organizations to approach IT more strategically, identify overlooked opportunities, and ultimately achieve superior performance in the digitized economy.

Besides such empirical findings, more theoretical research in IT governance has clearly advocated the importance of IT governance communications to external stakeholders of the firm [10, 31]. This theoretical underpinning, rooted in voluntary disclosure theory and agency theory predicts that firms can improve their liquidity and firm valuation through better information intermediation, enhance market reputation, reduce litigation costs, and the cost of capital [29].

2.3.2   The State of Practice in Belgium

We have examined how non-executive boards are reporting on their accountability towards IT in their yearly report. It appears that, notwithstanding the pervasive role of IT, the disclosure on IT governance is still limited and rather focused on reactive elements, for example when IT-related risk events happened. During the research more reporting was observed in high IT intense sectors as well as in public listed companies, the latter probably to be explained by the fact that investors might be willing to invest more in organizations that have their digitized assets under control. We believe that as the dependency on IT will continue to grow within all industries, IT governance disclosure might well become a critical piece of the non-financial information in most annual reports. As such, boards will become increasingly incentivized to disclose on the matter, with them increasing their own expectations towards executive management. Our research will supply examples from the field for boards and executive management to set up and operate an adequate disclosure strategy.

In order to gain insight in current IT governance disclosure practices, we analyzed the publicly available annual reports of 12 Belgian companies. We expected the non-financial information on these reports to contain information on IT governance practices as part of the overall corporate governance measures. The framework used to determine the rate and content of the IT governance disclosure is the one recently proposed in academic literature by Joshi et al. [32]. This disclosure framework proposed that non-executive boards can report on four areas of concern, more specifically IT Strategic Alignment, IT Value Delivery, IT Risk Management and IT Performance Management. As the IT governance disclosure rate will unavoidably vary among the companies selected, we clustered the companies to deduct whether organization within transform industries, where IT profoundly alters traditional ways of doing business by redefining business processes and relationships, disclose more on IT governance as opposed to organization in non-transform industries. Secondly, we analyzed whether those that are publicly listed disclose more than those that are not, because they are incentivized to do so by the market. While testing both propositions, we captured examples of language and narratives that could be considered as a good practice of IT governance disclosure.

With regard to the rate and content of IT governance disclosure, we were interested to know which topics make it into the annual reports and which don't. To have a canvas to score the reports against, we used the previously mentioned IT governance disclosure framework. This framework identified four domains on which can be reported in the annual statement: IT strategic alignment, IT value delivery, IT risk management and IT performance measurement. In each of these domains, expected reporting items were derived from literature. For example, in the domain of IT risk management, items on e.g. the "information security plan and policy" were expected, in IT Performance management explicit information in e.g. IT expenditure was captured, for IT value management elements on e.g. IT project updates were sought and for IT strategic alignment information was searched regarding e.g. the position of the CIO and existence of an IT steering committee. We looked at reporting rates, hence these results are by no means an indication of what really was present in the organization, only what was reported upon. In what follows we will explain the main observations from the research.

In general, we observed a low average reporting rate on IT governance. Firms report most in the domains of 'IT risk management' and their 'IT performance measurement'. Surprisingly, 'IT strategic alignment' is the least-disclosed category among the organizations in the sample. Overall, these results indicate that there is room for improvement in overall IT governance transparency in annual reports. Academic literature clearly suggests potential benefits of disclosure on non-financial aspects in general and IT-governance related aspects in specific, providing firms with a clear incentive to consider increasing their IT governance disclosure.

IT Strategic Alignment

'IT strategic alignment' deals with the fact that IT investments need to support the strategic goals and objectives of an organization in order to enable the creation of current and future business value. For IT strategic alignment topics, we observed an 8% average reporting rate. In one out of three cases there was a CIO or equivalent position in the firm, in 8% this position is on the executive board. In one out of four cases, we observed that IT risk is addressed at the audit or risk committee. If an IT committee was present, it was always established at the executive level.

> The ICT Board is the risk committee on IT matters. It comprises managing directors, two members of the Executive Board and the Chief Information Officer of Delta Lloyd Group.
>
> —Delta Lloyd

This surprisingly low result on IT strategic alignment disclosure is supported by Nolan and McFarlan [24] who stated that boards are often not aware of the importance of IT when it comes to supporting corporate objectives and the need for alignment between the overall corporate strategy and the IT strategy.

IT Value Delivery

'IT value delivery' is concerned with the optimization of IT-enabled value creation, where value is broader than strictly monetary (e.g. competitive advantage, higher employee productivity, etc.). These topics received attention in 24% of the reports. In half of the observed cases, IT was explicitly projected as a strength for the enterprise in achieving business objectives. In 42% of cases, the report stipulated that IT still is an opportunity for the enterprise, which might be an underestimation in this digital era.

> The new strategy is in line with ING's vision that technology and innovation play a crucial role in the future of ING Bank.
>
> —ING

With regard to IT projects, 33% of the reports gave an update on the status of projects (with 25% in a dedicated section). Green IT and IT sourcing decisions received attention in only 17% of cases, of which the latter can be explained because of a reluctance to disclose outsourcing to stakeholders. Absent from the equation are any suggestions made by the board on IT or any kind of framework by which IT is operating such as ITIL, COBIT or an ISO standard. This could indicate that the board is not shaping how value is delivered through IT, even though certainly at an operational level the best practices are set out by a variety of frameworks.

IT Risk Management

'IT risk management' is concerned with the protection of IT assets and recovery from IT-related disasters. From the four categories, IT risk management scores the best at an average 35%. IT is established as part of the operational risk in 58% of cases, although only 25% mentions a special IT risk management program. An information security plan is present in 67% of cases, but the business continuity aspects are only mentioned in one out of four reports. With regard to auditing, IT is covered in 25% of cases. Towards general regulation and compliance, IT is used in only 17% of cases.

> Other key action points during the year included significantly increasing the number of systematic analyses of the Group's potential information systems risks in order to assess the effectiveness of the internal control system, and rolling out to the shared service centers an internal control self-assessment method called 'World Class Administration'.
>
> —Saint-Gobain

There seems to be an underestimation of the business risk an IT incident might imply in terms of business continuity or compliance. As IT brings similar risks to all enterprises and might seriously impact the value of the firm, the overall rating of 35% on the IT risk management domain can be considered as too low. We know investors are concerned with IT security and as such this will influence their decision-making.

The security of online transactions is something to which Keytrade Bank pays a great deal of attention. It continues to invest in this aspect and seeks to offer its clients guaranteed security without compromising the efficiency of the transactions or the user-friendliness of the platform.

—Keytrade Bank

IT Performance Measurement

'IT performance measurement' is related to the IT budget and IT investments. It is specifically concerned with the expenditure on IT resources and its association to business value. The average disclosure rate of 32% is mainly due to the fact IT related assets are mentioned under intangible assets in 83% of cases, as imposed by IAS for listed companies.

Both purchased and internally-developed software are recognized as other intangible assets, but the latter only qualifies if it is identifiable that Delta Lloyd Group has the power to exercise control over the software and if the software will generate positive future cash flows.

—Delta Lloyd

There is also explicit information on IT expenditure in 67% of cases. Interestingly enough, the IT budget is never disclosed, nor is the direct cost on IT ever mentioned in currency or percentage.

Main Findings

Organizations in transform industries disclose more on IT governance as opposed to organizations in non-transform industries

As mentioned before, the role of IT within the industry (transform vs. non-transform) could have an impact on the IT governance disclosure rate. By comparing transform and non-transform groups of companies while keeping their reporting context the same (all listed companies in Belgium), we were able to determine a difference in the overall disclosure rate. Transform listed companies had an average reporting rate of 35% whereas non-transform listed companies were at 14%. These transform companies mainly deal with digital information, leading to the fact that information intensity is greater in these sectors [33]. For these companies, IT was always projected as a strength in the annual reports, and an information security plan was always mentioned. In 75% of cases, IT was mentioned as a strategic business issue, but also explicitly mentioned for achieving business objectives. Both the opportunity and risk perspective of IT are therefore clearly addressed for transform companies.

> *Listed companies disclose more IT governance information as opposed to non-listed companies.*
>
> With an overall disclosure rate of 35–26% (all transform industries Belgian companies), listed companies have an overall better disclosure rate than non-listed. Reasons can be found in prior research which states that disclosing non-financial information can improve a firm's valuation on the stock market. This incentivizes companies to explicitly mention practices with a known valuation impact such as having a dedicated CIO [34] or investing in IT (when in a transform industry) [35].

2.3.3   A Call for Action for Governing Boards

When considering the potential valuation impact of IT and the relatively unexplored nature of IT governance transparency, this type of research can be valuable to governing boards and executive committees to establish the right questions towards their direct reports. Chances are high that more practices are in place, but not reported on, which is a missed opportunity to convince stakeholders of the governance system. Formalized practices will enable boards and executive committees to take preventive action, as well as to detect deficiencies and take mitigating action, enabling them to show they are indeed in control of IT at a strategic level.

Our research on the annual reports of Belgian companies showed that IT governance disclosure is generally rather low and might be indicative of the IT governance maturity at executive and/or non-executive level. As IT risks and IT opportunities are ever-increasing and stakeholders rely on the non-financial information given to them to value the firm, boards and executive committees are incentivized to take up their IT governance role to be able to report on it.

2.4   Conclusion

In order to support boards of directors in their task to guide their organization in the digital age, we propose a roadmap consisting of three core tasks: install, measure and report. This roadmap provides a starting point for boards wanting to increase their engagement in governing digital assets and seeking clear and applicable guidance on how to implement this type of involvement.

The first task "install" entails the design and implementation of an appropriate IT governance system. Boards should first determine the role of IT in their organization in order to adapt the IT governance system accordingly. Then, the appropriate governance structures, such as an IT strategy and oversight committee, should be established. We provide specific guidelines on the workings of possible structures. On top of that, the board should ask critical questions with regard to IT in order to ensure that digital assets are properly governed and managed. Multiple examples of such questions were provided.

Measuring the various elements and outcomes of the established governance system is critical to ensure its effectiveness. We created a board-level dashboard for digital strategy and oversight to support boards of directors in this task. The dashboard covers four IT governance perspectives that should be monitored, i.e. future orientation, internal practices, stakeholders' orientation and corporate contribution.

Lastly, the board should report on their involvement in governing IT to external stakeholders. Given the continuing growth of organization dependence on IT, we believe IT governance disclosure could become a critical piece of the non-financial information in annual reports. Four focus areas of IT governance are provided which could be included in such reporting: IT strategic alignment, IT value delivery, IT risk management and IT performance measurement.

Chapter 3
Why Should Boards Care?

3.1 The Benefits of Board IT Governance

Digital transformation is all around us as numerous organizations increasingly rely on IT for the creation of business value. As a result, business strategy is more and more intertwined with IT strategy and risks coming from IT have gained importance. At the same time, boards of directors are ultimately accountable for strategic decision-making and control. Hence, it makes sense that boards of directors should take accountability for governing digital assets. With this in mind, we expect that organizations with boards involved in governing IT will reap the benefits in terms of strategic alignment, IT value delivery and risk management, which will ultimately translate into increased organizational performance.

Indeed, academic research shows that a higher level of board-level IT governance leads to increased organizational performance [12, 23, 36]. In these studies, the financial performance is measured using perceptions of directors concerning the firm's financial performance and its relative performance standing in its industry [12, 36] and perceptions of the degree to which IT contributes to (1) return on investment, (2) sales revenue increase, (3) market share increase, (4) cost savings, (5) operating efficiency, (6) process improvement and (7) customer satisfaction [23].

Strategic alignment plays an important role in the relationship between board-level IT governance and organizational performance. It concerns the level of alignment between the business and IT strategy, or in other words, to which extent the mission, objectives and plans of the business and IT strategy support each other. Strategic alignment has been a well-researched topic in IT governance research as it is found to be correlated with organizational performance. Recently, research has shown that board-level IT governance has a positive effect on strategic alignment [36], supporting our claim that board-level IT governance is positively linked with organizational performance. Indeed, board-level IT governance has both a direct positive relationship with organizational performance and an indirect relationship, through strategic alignment (Fig. 3.1) [12, 23, 36].

© Springer Nature Switzerland AG 2020

S. De Haes et al., *Governing Digital Transformation*, Management for Professionals,

https://doi.org/10.1007/978-3-030-30267-2_3

Fig. 3.1 Board-level IT
governance consequences—
conceptual model

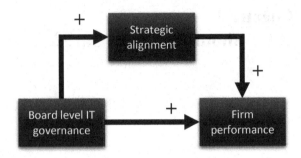

Boards can also improve firm valuation through IT governance transparency. Theoretical research has advocated the importance of IT governance communications to external stakeholders of the firm [10]. This theoretical underpinning, rooted in voluntary disclosure theory and agency theory, predicts that firms can improve their liquidity and firm valuation through better information intermediation. In highly digitized environment, transparency on IT governance can indeed be an important source of information for investors and other stakeholders.

3.2   How Does IT Fit into the Board's Duties?

The board can contribute to governing digital assets in different ways. These different contributions highlight the importance of such board involvement in IT governance. Building on organizational theories, the following key factors are identified explaining "how" boards should be involved in IT governance (Fig. 3.2).

Fig. 3.2 Summary of how IT
governance fits into the
board's duties

IT governance and the board's duties		
Provide oversight on IT related matters	Provide guidance and direction on IT related matters	Build unique digital capabilities for competitiveness
agency theory	*stewardship theory*	*resource dependency theory* *resource-based view of the firm*

3.2.1   Provide Oversight on IT-Related Matters (Agency Theory)

Building on agency theory, the board should play an oversight role to address the so-called principal-agent problem. The agency theory defines two actors: the principal, who is the task-assigning actor, and the agent who is the task-executing actor. Due to the different levels of risk acceptance among the actors, the tasks assigned to the agent can be executed in a way that conflicts with the principal's interests. To avoid the self-interested behavior of the agent, governance mechanisms can be applied to provide oversight [37, 38]. In terms of the board-level IT governance, the agency problem can arise between the board and executive management. Executive management and more specifically the CIO are employed as an agent by the board to take up the day-to-day operation of the organization, including IT matters. To enable effective oversight, the board can set an IT policy, ask critical questions, establish an IT-related oversight committee etc.

3.2.2   Provide Guidance and Direction on IT-Related Matters (Stewardship Theory)

Stewardship theory postulates that, in contradiction to agency theory, the relationship of an organization's owners and management is built on trust and equal interests. The behavior of the stewards is aligned with those of the principals [39]. Given this perspective, "managers need less oversight, and more advice, because they are deemed to be trustworthy good stewards of the resources they manage" [12]. In the context of board-level IT governance, this implies that it is the board's role to discuss IT issues and provide guidance to management based on these discussions.

3.2.3   Build Unique Digital Capabilities for Competitiveness (Resource Dependence Theory and Resource-Based View of the Firm)

According to resource dependence theory and the resource-based view of the firm, directors can be valuable resources both in terms of competencies and in terms of facilitating access to resources for the firm [40–42]. These resources can be internal or external to the organization [43]. In this context, the board can be a valuable resource in terms of knowledge and capital to the organization, acquired through industry experience. For example, board members can reuse IT oversight and guidance practices applied in other organizations or acquired through outsourcing experiences [12, 44]. As such, IT governance competencies at board level improves organizational performance by means of building unique (difficult to copy) board-level digital capabilities as an enabler for competiveness and sustainable growth [12].

3.3 Conclusion

In conclusion, as the ultimate goal of IT governance is the delivery of value from IT investments and IT risk mitigation, it makes sense that it eventually translates into financial indicators. Indeed, research confirms that the involvement of the board in governing digital assets results in increased overall organizational performance. On top of that, board level IT governance is a driver for business/IT strategic alignment, which in turn supports IT value delivery. Communicating to external stakeholders on such board involvement might result in additional benefits as it can improve the valuation of the firm.

The board's IT-related duties perfectly fit within the widely accepted roles of the board of directors, the control, service and resource dependence roles. More specifically, the board should (1) provide oversight on IT-related matters, (2) provide guidance and direction on IT-related matters and (3) build unique digital capabilities for competitiveness.

Chapter 4
Learning from Peers

To inspire board members seeking IT governance guidance, we have examined organizations that established certain governance mechanisms to (partly) tackle this challenge. As such, boards members can learn from their peers and translate best practices of other organizations to their own context and environment. To meet this objective, an organization was selected that initiated several actions to increase the level of board involvement in IT governance, i.e. the University of Antwerp. In the first section, we show how the board of directors of the university implements its IT governance duties. The second section describes the link between this case study and the guidelines provided in this book.

4.1 The Case of the University of Antwerp

I need to think about the university in 20 years, IT in 20 years and the society in 20 years.

—Rector of the University of Antwerp

The University of Antwerp is a relatively young university, founded in 2003, fusing three separate university institutions that date back to 1965. Currently the university is responsible for the education of 20,367 students of 116 nationalities. The university staff consists of 5,398 people, including professors, assistants, researchers, education staff and administrative and technical staff. Its three core tasks are research, education and services.

The central governance structure at the University of Antwerp (Fig. 4.1) consists of the rector, 3 central governing bodies and 9 central advisory bodies. The rector is the university's highest academic official. He is appointed for a four-year term by the board of directors after university-wide elections. The central governing bodies include the board of directors, the executive board and the board of administration, which is responsible for the daily management of the university. These governing

© Springer Nature Switzerland AG 2020
S. De Haes et al., *Governing Digital Transformation*, Management for Professionals,
https://doi.org/10.1007/978-3-030-30267-2_4

Fig. 4.1 Central governance structure at the University of Antwerp

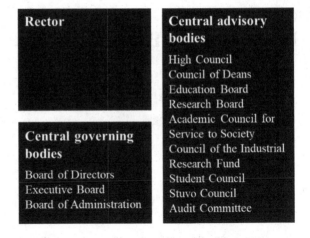

Rector	Central advisory bodies
	High Council
	Council of Deans
	Education Board
	Research Board
	Academic Council for
Central governing bodies	Service to Society
	Council of the Industrial
	Research Fund
Board of Directors	Student Council
Executive Board	Stuvo Council
Board of Administration	Audit Committee

bodies are supported by the central advisory bodies, including the education board, the research board and the academic council for service to society.

The IT department of the University of Antwerp maintains, manages and develops the university's IT infrastructure. They provide solutions to support the three core tasks of the university: research, education and services, but also facilitate secondary processes such as administration and management. In addition, they provide direct support to end-users and attend to the maintenance of the infrastructure.

4.2 Why Did the University of Antwerp Initiate Board-Level Involvement in Digital Strategy and Oversight?

Like many organizations, the University of Antwerp has become increasingly dependent on IT. This increasing dependence on IT also entails a growing number of IT-enabled investments that need to be carried out by the IT department. The IT department began to struggle with this great number of IT-enabled investments. No central business forum existed to decide which projects would be executed and which would not, swamping the IT department with many requests they could not deliver against. This situation often led to frustration at business side, a tension which was also reported to and known by some board members.

Furthermore, in 2016, a new rector came at the head of the University of Antwerp. The newly appointed rector strongly believes that the organization should think about long-term developments and how the university can adapt to these developments. More specifically, he stated that he thinks it is the task of the board of directors to create this long-term vision, also regarding IT-related issues.

Accordingly, the University of Antwerp decided to tackle the need to (1) establish a more formal IT portfolio management process that includes all relevant stakeholders, (2) increase the involvement of the board in this process and (3) ensure a more forward-looking approach. Two committees at the level of the board were created that discuss IT-related topics and an IT portfolio management process was established to align the IT project portfolio with the overall organization strategy.

4.3   How Did the University of Antwerp Initiate More Board-Level Involvement in Digital Strategy and Oversight?

4.3.1   Guiding Principles

When the University of Antwerp decided to act on the growing need for IT governance mechanisms, a set of guiding principles was agreed upon. These principles include:

1. Transparency regarding **investment criteria**: the evaluation of proposed investments should be handled in a transparent way. Clear criteria should be created to decide whether or not to start an investment.
2. Transparency regarding the **investment budget**: the size of the investment budget should be known at all times.
3. Transparency regarding **individual investments**: for every investment a business case needs to be developed according to a standard form. Moreover, a business owner is appointed to each investment and no investments can be launched without a business owner.
4. Transparency regarding the **investment portfolio**: all investments need to go through the same portfolio decision cycle so that a full and transparent view can be obtained.

These guiding principles were used as a basis to create the board-level IT governance structures and processes that will be described in the following sections.

4.3.2   Governing Structures

A widely acknowledged strategy to increase and improve the involvement of the board in IT-related decision making and control, is to enhance its IT expertise [9, 20, 23]. However, due to the nature of the board of directors at the university, there are not many options to thoughtfully alter its composition. When the University of Antwerp initiated more board level engagement in digital strategy and oversight, only 6 of the 25 members of the board were external directors. The internal directors were appointed after elections among the different university entities and students. From the 6 external members, the university could merely appoint 3. The others were selected by the minister for education, the governor of the province of Antwerp and the provincial superior of the society of Jesus, which made it difficult to increase the level of IT expertise among board members. Since September 1st, 2017, the board is allowed to appoint 3 additional directors. This change will provide the university with the opportunity to slightly alter the composition of the board. As the 3 additional members have not been appointed yet at the time of writing, the future will show whether this new arrangement will result in a higher level of IT expertise at the board of directors.

Due to the limited level of IT expertise on the board, it makes sense to make sure this IT expertise is present and IT-related debates are held in other structures that report to or advise the board. Accordingly, committees were created that include board members and that assist the board in IT-related decision making and control. Indeed, the creation of an IT oversight or similar committee at board level is a frequently mentioned approach in academic literature to increase board involvement in IT governance [12, 24, 45]. At the university, two such committees were created (Fig. 4.2). One committee, the IT governance committee, considers rather short-term decisions and is in charge of portfolio management of IT-enabled investments. The other committee, the digital strategy think tank, considers the long term from more an outside-in perspective.

4.3.2.1   IT Governance Committee and Investment Office

The IT governance committee was established in 2015 and meets 3 times a year. The main goal of this committee is to manage the IT-enabled investment portfolio more effectively and transparently and make sure it is in line with the overall organization strategy. From a board's perspective, the committee should provide reasonable assurance that the university's IT-enabled investments are in line with its strategy. Indeed, up until now, the main topic of the committee meetings has been which investments to execute. However, the interviewees indicated that in the future, other topics like project benefits delivery and the IT policy plan could be part of this meeting.

Fig. 4.2 Board-level IT governance structures at the University of Antwerp

Not all IT-enabled investments pass by the IT governance committee. Rather operational investments—like the renewal of certain academic software licenses—are not discussed at this level of the organization, as these would overburden this forum. Instead, the committee focusses on more strategic and innovative projects, which cover about 45% of the entire IT budget.

Due to the democratic nature of the decision-making culture at the university, it is crucial to include a broad delegation of people of the university in this committee. Hence, the goal was to create an entity that would represent all university entities as good as possible. The result is a committee that consists of 15 voting members and 30 advisory members. In addition, the chairman and vice-chairman can invite internal or external experts that act as advisors. The 15 voting members are:

- Rector (chairman)
- Chair of the Board of Administration (vice-chairman)
- The 4 vice-rectors
- 3 Members of the board of directors
- 3 Members appointed by the Council of Deans
- 2 Heads of the IT department

The composition reveals that the board is actively engaged in the IT debate. Four directors were appointed voting members of the IT governance committee (including the rector) and all other directors are also welcome to join. Indeed, at the past committee meetings, attendance ranged from 4 up to 8 directors.

As the heads of the IT department are included in the committee, a certain level of IT expertise is present. However, the goal of the committee is not to go too much into the technical details, but to discuss the investments from a business perspective. Of course, the details must be considered at one point. Therefore, it was decided to establish an additional preparatory committee; the investment office.

The investment office has the responsibility to prepare investments to be presented to the IT governance committee. The investment office evaluates these investments from a business, technical and risk perspective, using a scoring model (see also the section on "processes"). It does not make any investment decisions but can conclude that a proposed investment is not yet fully defined and matured in the current business case document. As it has a more in-depth focus, it is made up of fewer members. Still, the goal is to represent the entire university as good as possible. More specifically, the investment office consists of:

- Chair of the Board of Administration (chairman)
- Heads of the three core boards (the Education Board, the Research Board and the Academic Council for Service to Society)
- Coordinator Administrative Simplifications Office
- 2 Heads of the IT department
- Professor IT governance.

4.3.2.2   Digital Strategy Think Tank

The other IT governance structure at the top-level of the university is the digital strategy think tank. The current rector started his term in 2016. From the beginning of his mandate, he stated he wants *"an organization that is agile and thinks about future needs"* and in support of that, he wants to free up the time of the board to execute this task. In light of these developments, he initiated the creation of the digital strategy think tank which meets several times a year (the meeting frequency is undefined, in 2017 already 4 meetings took place). The goal of this committee is to consider long term developments that could influence the university. They consider both how emerging technologies can impact the university's business model and strategy, as well as how challenges in society and markets could be addressed levering new technological innovations. One of the topics discussed was the fact that at a certain point in the future, more people will retire than enter the job market, which might trigger companies to hire students before they have finished their masters. This development could affect the university, as it might require students to obtain their master's degree in a more flexible way, for example supported by e-learning. These kind of digital strategy discussions require a certain level of IT expertise, which is reflected in the composition of the committee. The members of the digital strategy think tank are:

- Rector
- Chair of the Board of Administration
- 3 professors with IT expertise
- A board member with IT expertise
- 4 members of the IT department

Similar to the IT governance committee, the board of directors is represented in the think tank; the rector and one other board member are included. The difference is that for the digital strategy think tank, they specifically opted to include a board member with IT expertise.

4.3.3   Governing Processes

Each IT-enabled investment must follow the process as depicted in Fig. 4.3. The process consists of three stages: (1) investment description, to get a basic idea of what the investment is about, (2) investment scoring, to evaluate the investment in an objective way and (3) the investment decision, when a decision is made on whether or not to execute the investment. The goal of this process is to create an IT-enabled investment portfolio that is consistent with the organization strategy.

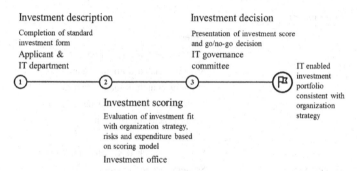

Fig. 4.3 IT-enabled investment life cycle at the University of Antwerp

4.3.3.1 Investment Description

Every investment needs to have a dedicated (business) initiator who signs of the investment description. In order to fully grasp the idea and corresponding workload of an investment, this initiator needs to complete a standard form or mini business case. The IT department is available to assist any applicant in completing this form, although it remains the accountability of the business initiator to fill in the template. Even though this pre-assessment requires a certain effort, any problems in a later stage might be prevented. Moreover, this pre-assessment allows for a certain type of triage, making sure that the IT governance committee does not become overloaded. That is, if this pre-assessment reveals that an investment requires less than a month of work, it does not have to pass by the investment office and IT governance committee and will simply be executed.

4.3.3.2 Investment Scoring

> It is important to look at the goals of the organization and evaluate whether IT supports the attainment of these goals.
>
> —Head of the IT department of the University of Antwerp

When the standard form is completed, the investment is presented to the investment office. Here, the fit with the organization strategy, the risks and the expenditure will be evaluated based on a scoring model, enabling a fairly objective quotation of the investment. Investments are evaluated from a business as well as a technical perspective. For example, the match with the three core tasks of the university (education, research and services) is assessed. An overview of all the scoring criteria is shown in Table 1. For each of these criteria, underlying questions were developed that allow to come to a "green", "yellow" or "red" score in a consistent way. Green represents a good match, yellow exemplifies a limited match and red suggests there is no match. In case the investment criterion is not applicable (e.g. an investment in

Table 1 Scoring model

Domain	Criteria
Business domain	Strategic match domain education
	Strategic match domain research
	Strategic match domain services
	Administrative streamlining
	Management information
	Marketing/image
	Strategic match ICT policy plan
Technology domain	Strategic IS architecture
	Definitional uncertainty
	Technical uncertainty
	IS infrastructure risk

a new online platform for education is not relevant for the education strategy) a "grey" score is used. At the end of this exercise, a scorecard is created, showing the benefits, risks and expenditure of each investment. The scores are presented using colors, as this enables the reader to evaluate the investment's strengths and weaknesses at a glance.Scoring model

This scoring model does not represent classic estimators like return on investment (ROI) or net present value (NPV), which was a deliberate choice. One of the heads of the IT department argues that *"it is more important to look at the goals of the organization and evaluate whether IT supports the attainment of these goals."* That is exactly what this scoring model is used for.

4.3.3.3 Investment Decision

At this point, a decision needs to be made on whether or not the investment will be executed. This decision is made by the IT governance committee. The investment and its scores as developed by the investment office are presented to the IT governance committee in an understandable and non-technical way. The investment is briefly summarized by the business owner and then discussed in the IT governance committee referring to the investment criteria scores; However, in principle, the scores are not debated anymore. Indeed, no debate has been held on the scores of an investment during an IT governance committee meeting so far. At the end of the discussion a go/no-go decision is reached.

Key Takeaways
This case study contributed to answering the research question that was put forward: "How can boards operationalize their role in digital strategy and oversight?". It described the situation of a specific organization and how it combined several IT governance mechanisms in order to engage the board of directors in digital strategy and oversight.

The University of Antwerp established several structures and processes at the level of the board of directors in order to increase the involvement of the board in IT governance, establish a formal and transparent IT portfolio management process and ensure a long-term view on digital aspects.

Three new structures were created. The IT governance committee that is responsible for managing the IT-enabled investment portfolio in a more effective and transparent way and making sure all IT-enabled investments are in line with the overall organization strategy. This committee is supported by the investment office. The investment office prepares investment proposals and the investment decision process. The digital strategy think tank is tasked with discussing digital developments in the long run. Board members are included in both the IT governance committee and the digital strategy think tank.

Each IT-enabled investment follows the same portfolio management process. This process consists of three steps. First, a mini business case is created for the investment by its business owner. Second, based upon this business case, the investment office evaluates the investment from a business, technical and risk perspective, using an agreed-upon scoring model. The last step consists of presenting this score to the IT governance committee, which makes a go/no-go decision.

The University of Antwerp case is interesting as it sheds a light on how to deal with the specifics, more specifically the constraints, of an organization and adapt the board-level IT governance mechanisms accordingly.

This case illustrates that even with a board consisting of primarily elected members and a culture of creating support in the entire organization before taking any decisions, the board can actively participate in the digital debate. Their solution consists of the creation of two committees supporting the board in this task that include adequate IT expertise and directors as members.

Additionally, it shows that the tone at the top, in this case through the rector, can significantly impact the governance structures. The rector strongly believes that the university should be more forward-looking, thinking about long term developments. *"I need to think about the university in 20 years, IT in 20 years and the society in 20 years."* This vision was also translated to IT, with the creation of the digital strategy think tank.

4.4   Realizing the Value of Board-level IT Governance

In this section, we will re-interpret the case of the University of Antwerp through the lens of our earlier described guidance. This analysis will shed a light on how this guidance can be used to realize the value of board level IT governance.

4.4.1 Task 1: Install

We have suggested three steps in order to build digital leadership capabilities for the board. First, the board should articulate an understanding of the role of IT in the organization. Second, the appropriate governance structures should be established and finally, the board should give direction and provide oversight by asking critical questions. In 2016, the University of Antwerp initiated the creation of IT governance structures and processes at the level of the board in order to increase their engagement in IT-related strategic decision-making and control. The established governance practices are fully in line with the aforementioned recommendations, as we will demonstrate in the next paragraphs.

4.4.1.1 Step 1: Articulate an Understanding of the (Evolving) Role of IT in the Organization

A first step consists of defining the role of IT in the organization. The toolkit recommends the application of the strategic impact grid of Nolan and McFarlan [24]. This framework identifies four "IT use modes" based on the organization's need for reliable IT and its need for new IT. We argue that the need for reliable IT of the University of Antwerp is currently rather low. Even though a failure of IT systems would have a certain impact on the university, most core business processes relating to education and research will be able to continue. Regarding the need for new IT, the university is going through an evolution. In the past, the university's need for new IT was rather low as it did not rely on IT for its competitiveness. However, concepts like e-learning and blended learning are increasingly adopted, creating increased competition among universities worldwide. On top of that, digital natives are now the university's main target audience. They might opt for a university with clear digital offerings, like the possibility of remote learning. In order to stay competitive, we expect the University of Antwerp shall need to offer more digital learning solutions in the future. In this regard, the need for new IT might evolve from rather low to high, putting the University of Antwerp in turnaround mode in the future. Important to note is that the turnaround mode is a transition state. Usually organizations quickly move to strategic mode, as an increased need for new IT in many cases results in an increase of the need for reliable IT [24]. Hence, we conclude that in the University of Antwerp the role of IT is changing, evolving from an organization in support mode to one in turnaround mode. Ultimately, the university will end up in strategic mode.

4.4.1.2 Step 2: Establish the Appropriate Governance Structures

In order to realize this transition from support to strategic mode, the board also needs to change its governing processes and structures around the digital assets. For organizations with a low need for new IT, the audit and/or risk committee can take up the IT oversight role. However, there is a risk of inadequate focus on IT issues, as the responsibilities of these committees are typically of limited scope. On the other hand, organizations in turnaround or strategic mode could opt for increasing the IT expertise in the board and systematically putting IT-related topics on the agenda or for this task to be taken over by an IT strategy and oversight committee at the level of the board.

As there is not a "silver bullet" IT governance model [46], the context of the organization should be taken into account when deciding on the appropriate governance structures. Indeed, three important elements of the situation of the University of Antwerp determined the final composition of governance practices. First, the main issue that led the university to initiate the board-level IT governance implementation was the lack of alignment of the IT portfolio with the overall business strategy due to the absence of a formal IT portfolio management process and a lack of involvement of the board. Second, the university's board of directors mainly consists of members elected among the different university entities. As a consequence, there is not much room to increase IT expertise in the board by thoughtfully altering its composition. Third, a new rector was elected in 2016. He strongly felt that the board should free up more time to create a long-term vision, also regarding IT.

Given this situation, it made sense to create an IT governance committee in support of the board of directors. Its main responsibilities are the effective and transparent management of the IT-enabled investment portfolio and the alignment of IT with the overall organization strategy. The committee includes representatives of all university entities, among which four directors. All other directors are always welcome to join. The IT governance committee first met on the 26th of February, 2016. In addition, the rector initiated the creation of the digital strategy think tank. This is a smaller committee, consisting of ten members, of which two are board members. Its responsibility is to keep an eye on the impact of technological developments on the university and consider how societal and market challenges could be addressed leveraging technology. The think tank is a relatively new initiative, as its first meeting was held on the 14th of March, 2017.

4.4.1.3 Step 3: Give Direction and Provide Oversight by Asking Critical Questions

Once the roles and responsibilities are allocated, the board should ask the "right" questions in order to perform its control and advising functions. Depending on the role of IT in the organization, the questions in Fig. 2.5 were suggested.

As we argued the university is currently in support mode and evolving towards turnaround mode, the questions in the lower quadrants should therefore be asked. Indeed, questions about the changing role of IT in the organization and the actions of competitors are discussed in the digital strategy think tank. The question "Do we have processes in place that will enable us to discover and execute any strategic IT opportunity" is addressed in the IT governance committee. Our claim that the university will ultimately end up in strategic mode appears to be acknowledged by the university itself, as the IT governance committee already addresses one of the questions in the upper right quadrant "Are our strategic IT development plans proceeding as required?"

4.4.2   Task 2: Measure

A board-level dashboard for digital strategy and oversight was created that boards can use to monitor their effectiveness in taking up a digital leadership role. This dashboard consists of four perspectives boards should monitor: corporate contribution, stakeholders' orientation, internal practices and future orientation. For each of these perspectives, a mission and more specific objectives were specified. For each objective, specific metrics were created that can be used to monitor the level of achievement.

Since there is no best way for boards to engage in IT governance, it makes sense that the measurement of their effectiveness in doing so differs between different types of organizations. Therefore, the dashboard takes into account the role of IT in the organization based on the strategic impact grid of Nolan and McFarlan [24]. This is in line with the previous toolkit, thus, boards can effortlessly combine both toolkits.

The dashboard can be applied, as a lens, to the case of the University of Antwerp, in order to evaluate which metrics are influenced by the increased engagement of the board in digital oversight. Since we argued the university is currently evolving from support to turnaround mode, we should focus on the metrics relating to these two modes. An overview of these metrics is shown in Figs. 4.4–4.7. Even though the board-level IT governance initiatives at the university of Antwerp are still in their early stages, we believe that they have a certain impact on several of these metrics.

The **future orientation** perspective (Fig. 4.4) is considered to be the foundation of futureproof board-level IT governance. The objectives included in this perspective relate to skills and knowledge and culture. As the composition of the board of directors at the university does not facilitate the development of IT expertise among board members, this objective and its relating metric are not significantly impacted. We do expect that the metrics relating to culture are influenced by the board-level IT governance initiatives taken at the university. An increase of the level of awareness of IT strategic importance among board members is highly plausible for three reasons. First, the creation of the IT governance committee was approved by the board of directors after a presentation of the IT policy plan by the head of the IT department. This policy plan extensively describes the role of IT in the organization. By approving the creation of this governing body, the board of directors implicitly acknowledged the strategic importance of IT. Second, four board members are officially included in the IT governance committee. In this committee, it is clearly shown how IT fits into the business strategy. Furthermore,

Fig. 4.4 Board-level dashboard—Future orientation at the University of Antwerp

	Mission	Objectives	Board metrics	Support	Turnaround
Future orientation	Building foundations for IT governance delivery	Skills and knowledge	Percentage of board members with expertise related to mangement or governance of IT		x
		Culture	Level of awareness of IT strategic importance among board members / organization's dependence on IT	x	x
			Level of awareness of the board's role in IT governance	x	x
			Number of board directives that discuss the role of IT in the organzation		x

all other board members are welcome to join. Indeed, at the past committee meetings, attendance ranged from four up to eight board members. Third, the rector is the one that initiated the creation of the digital strategy think tank, which clearly demonstrates the importance of this topic for the university. Obviously, the inclusion of board members in both newly created IT governing bodies confirms the role of the board in IT governance. In conclusion, the foundations for IT governance delivery are strengthened, primarily through raising the level of awareness of IT strategic importance among board members and their role in IT governance.

The second perspective concerns the **internal practices**, ensuring effective and sustained IT governance (Fig. 4.5). The focus of the board level IT governance initiatives at the University of Antwerp is clearly placed on structures. With the creation of the IT governance committee and the digital strategy think tank, the metrics "number of meetings of IT strategy and oversight committee" and "level of attendance of board members to IT strategy and oversight committee" are unmistakably positively influenced. The IT governance committee meets three times a year. The official number of meetings of the digital strategy think tank a year is still undefined. In 2017, they met four times. The level of attendance of board members to the IT governance committee ranges from four to eight directors. On average one board member was present at the meetings of the digital strategy think tank. We expect the attendance level to the think tank meetings will increase, as this is a newly created structure, still searching for its modus operandi.

Board-level IT governance processes were not the focus of the university's board. Nevertheless, we expect to see a certain increase in some of the process-related metrics. That is, we expect the "percentage of time spent on IT innovation topics during board meetings" and the "number of times IT innovation

Fig. 4.5 Board-level dashboard—Internal practices at the University of Antwerp

Internal practices	Ensuring effective and sustained IT governance	Mission	Objectives		Board metrics	IT use mode	
						Support	Turnaround
				Structures	Number of meetings of IT strategy and oversight committee		x
					Level of attendance of board members to IT strategy and oversight committee		x
				Processes	Number of times IT is an item on the audit committee agenda	x	
					Percentage of time spent on IT innovation topics during board meetings		x
					Number of times IT innovation topics are items on the board meeting agenda		x
					Frequency of suggestions/decisions/advise by the board on IT		x
					Number of presentations from the CIO to the board		x

topics are items on the board meeting agenda" to grow. The digital strategy think tank has a strong focus on IT innovation. As it was only established in 2017, the board does not consider IT innovation topics more often yet. However, we expect the results of the discussions in the think tank to spark board discussions on IT innovation topics.

Both the future orientation and the internal practices perspective refer to what boards should do to ensure digital strategy and oversight. On the other hand, the stakeholders' orientation and corporate contribution refer to what boards can expect as outcome from their digital strategy and oversight. In other words, they measure the consequences of increased engagement of the board in IT governance.

The **stakeholders' orientation** mainly relates to transparency (Fig. 4.6). More specifically, the metric "level of disclosure on IT governance in annual reports" is identified. Contrarily to what we might expect, the level of transparency in the university's annual report has not increased. This can be explained by the fact that (1) the University of Antwerp typically publishes very brief annual reports and (2) the most recent annual report at the moment of writing is the one of 2016, the year in which the board deliberately and actively initiated the increase of their involvement in digital oversight. Hence, it might be too soon for these changes to be reflected in voluntary disclosure.

Fig. 4.6 Board-level dashboard—Stakeholders' orientation at the University of Antwerp

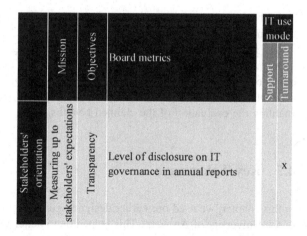

Stakeholders' orientation	Mission	Objectives	Board metrics	IT use mode	
				Support	Turnaround
	Measuring up to stakeholders' expectations	Transparency	Level of disclosure on IT governance in annual reports		x

Regarding **corporate contribution** (Fig. 4.7), the university mainly focuses on strategic alignment and value delivery, which is entirely in line with the recommendations for their IT use mode. As the alignment of IT with the overall organization strategy is the explicit responsibility of the IT governance committee, the fit between IT and business strategy is expected to increase. More specifically, the IT governance committee manages the IT-enabled investment portfolio and aligns it with the business strategy. Hence, we expect the percentage of IT development capacity engaged in strategic projects to increase. The metric that was identified with regard to value delivery is "the percent of IT-enabled investments where claimed benefits are met or exceeded". Currently, the IT governance committee does not yet track project benefits delivery, although project owners already need to

Fig. 4.7 Board-level dashboard—Corporate contribution at the University of Antwerp

Corporate contribution	Ensuring maximum value through IT with reasonable risk	Mission	Objectives	Board metrics	IT use mode	
					Support	Turnaround
			Strategic alignment	Level of alignment of business strategy with the distribution in the IT budget between IT investments and operations	x	x
				Percentage of IT development capacity engaged in strategic projects		x
				Fit between business strategy and IT strategy	x	x
			Value delivery	Percent of IT-enabled investments where claimed benefits are met or exceeded	x	x

report back to the committee intermediate status-report during the execution of the investment. Furthermore, with the creation of the IT governance committee, a formal IT investment process was defined. According to this process, a standard investment form needs to be completed for each IT-related investment that is proposed, including the definition of the expected project benefits. In the past, the description of such a business case was not required. Hence, this is a first step in enabling the evaluation of the claimed benefits.

4.5 Key Takeaways

In this chapter, we used our earlier designed guidance as a lens to analyze the case of the University of Antwerp. This helped us to better understand how board-level IT governance can lead to more value for the organization.

The board-level IT governance initiatives taken at the University of Antwerp are completely in line with the advice as designed in three-step approach to getting started with board-level IT governance. Their governance practices perfectly fit the role of IT in their organizations. More specifically, they created two structures at the level of the board, the IT governance committee and the digital strategy think tank, that are responsible for digital strategy and oversight. In these committees, the IT-related questions are addressed. Two interesting observations can be made. First, the case shows that the role of IT in the organization can be dynamic. That is, the university is currently going through an evolution from support mode, to turn-around mode, ultimately ending up in strategic mode. Second, the case confirms that the guidance should be adapted to the specific situation of the organization. The toolkit for example says that the appropriate governance structures should be established and suggests the creation of an IT strategy and oversight committee. At the university, it was decided to create two separate committees. One large committee including many university representatives, the IT governance committee, responsible for the alignment of the IT portfolio with the business strategy and one smaller committee, the digital strategy think tank, responsible for the long-term vision relating to IT.

Next, the effectiveness of the board of directors of the University of Antwerp in taking up their responsibilities relating to the governance of IT can be measured using the Board Level Dashboard for Digital Strategy and Oversight. We expect the governance initiatives to have a positive effect on metrics relating to the future orientation and internal practices. More specifically, the university's actions strengthen its culture with regard to the awareness of board members of their role in and the importance of IT-related matters. Furthermore, the university ensures effective and sustained IT governance by creating the right structures at the level of the board. As a result, we believe the metrics belonging to the corporate contribution perspective are positively influenced, with a specific focus on strategic alignment.

Academic research shows that higher levels of engagement of the board in IT governance are indeed related to increased organizational performance. A large part of this effect can be attributed to strategic alignment. Hence, we expect that when organizations apply the guidance provided in our toolkits, they will be able to reap the benefits in terms of organizational performance. Indeed, the case of the University of Antwerp sheds light on the consequences of applying these recommendations. In this case, strategic alignment is primarily impacted. Thus, with the academic research in mind, we expect that the university's initiatives will ultimately have a positive impact on its performance.

Chapter 5
Governance Objectives to Lead Digital Transformation

Chapter 2 of this book provides a generic roadmap for boards of directors towards governing digital transformation. The frequently used framework COBIT 2019 also addresses some elements of the involvement of the board in governing IT. The COBIT 2019 framework perfectly complements our roadmap as it allows us to provide a more elaborate discussion on certain parts of the roadmap.

In this chapter, the relevant COBIT governance objectives will be shortly introduced and discussed in more detail using related academic research.

5.1 COBIT 2019

Control Objectives for Information and Related Technology (COBIT), developed by the Information Systems Audit and Control Association (ISACA), is a framework for 'enterprise governance of information and technology (EGIT)'. The first version of this framework was released in 1996 (version 1), with updates in 1998 (version 2), 2000 (version 3), 2005 (version 4), 2007 (version 4.1), and 2012 (version 5). Over time, COBIT evolved into a mature good-practices framework for ensuring appropriate control over IT [47]. In November 2018 the successor of COBIT 5, i.e. COBIT 2019, was officially released. This most recent COBIT update is aimed at facilitating a more flexible, tailored implementation of effective 'enterprise governance of information and technology (EGIT)'.

The COBIT 2019 core model consists of 40 governance and management objectives (i.e. 5 governance and 35 management objectives) that assist enterprises in establishing appropriate control over their (current and future) use of IT (i.e. IT-enabled business projects, IT operations etc.) The achievement of these governance and management objectives contributes to an effective EGIT approach. The explicit distinction between governance and management objectives is driven by the recognition that a clear difference exists between the governance and management activities and the involved roles/structures in the context of EGIT. Indeed,

© Springer Nature Switzerland AG 2020
S. De Haes et al., *Governing Digital Transformation*, Management for Professionals,
https://doi.org/10.1007/978-3-030-30267-2_5

in most enterprises, governance is the responsibility of the board of directors under the leadership of the chairperson. Management is then responsible for planning, building, running, and monitoring activities, in alignment with the direction set by the governing body, to achieve the enterprise's goals. In most enterprises, management is the responsibility of the executive committee under the leadership of the chief executive officer. As such, COBIT's governance objectives essentially reflect the required involvement of the board of directors in the context of the governance of IT.

The (governance and management) objectives can be achieved by putting in place an EGIT system consisting of a number of components (i.e. processes; organizational structures and other related components). The COBIT 2019 framework provides guidance related to how to instantiate these components in order to achieve each of the objectives. The guidance related to the 'process' component provides insights on the process practices and hands-on activities that need to be performed in order to achieve the objective. The guidance related to the 'organizational structures' component deals with the roles and structures that are involved in the process and its containing process practices.

The following sections of this chapter discuss each of the 5 governance objectives contained in COBIT 2019. As such, a brief overview is provided of COBIT's guidance aimed at establishing effective and appropriate control over IT that is relevant for the board of directors.

5.2 Ensured Governance Framework Setting and Maintenance (EDM01)

Today's firms are increasingly using digital technologies for strategic purposes, accompanied by fundamentally reshaped (digital) business strategies [48]. IT is considered to be steadily growing into the largest capital expense of organizations [49]. As a result of this growing pervasiveness of IT, organizational decision-makers are increasingly facing important IT-related decisions at all managerial levels (i.e. operational, tactical, and strategic). Disciplines like IT management (more operationally-oriented) and IT governance (more strategically-oriented) developed to assist organizations with these issues and ensure appropriate control over their current and future IT use [50–52]. Putting in place and maintaining an IT governance framework with clear accountabilities and responsibilities has as such become a necessity for many organizations [50].

The first governance objective included in the COBIT 2019 framework, *ensured governance framework setting and maintenance*, is directly related to this issue. Through achieving this governance objective, the board ensures that the requirements for IT governance are analysed and articulated, and that an effective governance system is put in place and maintained so that there is a clarity of responsibilities and authority to achieve the organization's mission, goals and objectives. The actual setting and maintenance of the IT governance arrangement or framework is to be performed by executive management (i.e. responsibility), but the board of directors should ensure that this is indeed effectively performed (i.e. accountability).

A first important governance practice that is required to achieve this important governance objective is the continuous evaluation of the organization's IT governance. More specific tasks include: determining the implications of the organization's overall corporate governance for IT (and its governance); analysing and identifying (internal and external) factors (e.g. legal, regulatory and contractual obligations) that may influence the organization's IT governance framework; articulating principles for IT governance in the organization; and determining the role of IT for the organization.

The IT governance principles will guide the actual design and implementation of IT governance. As such, these principles will provide handholds to executive management in their responsibilities of putting in place and maintaining the organization's IT governance arrangement. Examples of principles used in real-life organizations are provided in Fig. 5.1.

A second key governance practice in the context of achieving this governance objective is informing other stakeholders on the articulated IT governance principles, obtaining their commitment, and guiding the design of the IT governance framework in line with the agreed-upon principles. More specific tasks include: agreeing with executive management on IT governance principles and communicating these principles throughout the organization; ensuring that the established IT governance arrangement is in line with these principles; and establishing an organizational structure at the level of the board of directors which is tasked with ensuring that IT governance is adequately addressed and that IT investment programs are in line with the business strategy and objectives.

As mentioned in Chap. 2 of this book, an organizational structure at the level of the board of directors could be a committee. Like other board-level committees (e.g. audit committee or compensation committee), such a committee (e.g. labeled "IT strategy committee", "IT oversight committee", or "IT governance committee") would comprise directors with specific expertise, and make specific recommendations to the board [18, 19, 24]. It is however extremely important that such a board-level committee *"[...] neither assumes the board's governance*

- IT is a professional organization that effectively and efficiently manages its resources in alignment with the needs of the organization.
- IT is the exclusive provider of IT services. Outsourcing is always organised in partnership between business and IT.
- IT is pro-actively engaged in further developing and innovating the organization.
- The priorities within IT are aligned to the strategic goals of the organizations through integrated planning cycles.

Fig. 5.1 Example IT governance principles [46]

accountability nor makes final decisions. Neither does it play a role in day-to-day management. It acts solely as an advisor to the board and management on current and future IT-related issues." [18]

The final governance practice put forward in the context of achieving this first governance objective is monitoring the effectiveness and performance of the organization's IT governance. More specific tasks include: periodically assessing if the agreed-upon IT governance mechanisms (i.e. structures, processes etc.) are established and performing effectively; identifying actions to rectify any deviations between the designed and implemented IT governance; and monitor the assessment of the extent to which the use of IT in the organization complies with relevant obligations (i.e. regulatory, legislation, common law, contractual), standards and guidelines.

Indeed, the activities of the organization in general, and its (current and future) IT use in specific, are required to comply with the constraints and obligations (e.g. regulatory and legal requirements) that are imposed upon the organization [18, 53]. There is an increasing amount of IT-related regulatory and legal requirements with which an organization needs to ensure compliance [17]. A recent example that is especially relevant in the context of IT governance is the General Data Protection Regulation (GDPR), which regulates the processing of personal data of individuals and is directly binding and applicable for all organizations established in the European Economic Area (EEA), or any organization that is processing personal data of individuals inside the EEA.

5.3   Ensured Benefits Delivery (EDM02)

The ultimate goal of IT governance is creating business value from IT-enabled business investments [46]. Indeed, the ITGI [18] identified value delivery as one of the focus areas of IT governance. But how to ensure such value delivery? The EDM governance objective provides some guidelines on how to "optimize the value to the business from investments in business processes, IT services and IT assets". In business terms, such value optimization will ultimately support the optimization of the internal business process functionality and the management of digital trans-formation programs.

In order to ensure value optimization from IT-related investments, COBIT 2019 proposes four governance practices. First, the target investment mix should be established, which balances costs and benefits, alignment with the overall strategy, risks, and financial measures (e.g. expected return on investment (ROI)). Second, the resulting portfolio should be continually evaluated with regard to its value delivery. Based on this assessment, changes should be made in direction to man-agement. Third, the board should oversee the management principles and practices that enable optimal value realization from IT-related investments throughout their full economic life cycle. This can be achieved by defining criteria and relative weightings to criteria to determine relative value scores, defining requirements for stage-gate reviews, etc. Lastly, value optimization from IT-enabled investments should be monitored by tracking key goals and metrics. Any significant discrepancies should be identified, and appropriate action should be taken.

But what exactly constitutes value from IT-related investments? This is a crucial question that should be answered to enable boards to actually ensure benefits delivery. Schryen [54] defines information systems (IS) business value as *"the impact of investments in particular IS assets on the multidimensional performance and capabilities of economic entities at various levels, complemented by the ultimate meaning of performance in the economic environment"*. An important notion in this definition is *the ultimate meaning of performance*. Boards should not only consider the direct outcome of an IT investment, but also what subsequently results from this outcome. For example, the productivity of employees might increase with the use of an enterprise resource planning (ERP) system. In order to evaluate the true value of such an investment, the organization should ask itself: how is the extra time these employees now have exploited? Did competitors experience such productivity gains as well? [54].

It is also important to note that in his definition, Schryen [54] takes a broad view of IS, not only taking into account hardware and software. That is, he considers IS to be *"the entire infrastructure, organization, personnel, and components for the collection, processing, storage, transmission, display, dissemination, and disposition of information"* [54].

Schryen [54] provides a taxonomy of IS business value that boards could use to determine what types of value could originate from IT-related investments, which in turn defines what should be monitored. The taxonomy includes two business value dimensions. The first one distinguishes between internal and competitive value. The second dimension separates tangible from intangible value.

Internal value stems from business process redesign, better decision-making, more flexible coordination and productivity gains enabled by IT-related investments. The taxonomy created by Schryen [54] includes IS assets, IS capabilities and socio-organizational capabilities as contributors to internal value from IT. IS capabilities entail the IS competencies of employees, the IS practices deployed by these employees and capabilities concerning the management of IS. Changes in these capabilities could contribute to internal value. Socio-organizational capabilities refer to the practices, processes and structures that evolve over time and as such trigger socio-organizational change. The internal value created by IS assets comes from the change in these assets and more specifically from IS innovation.

Internal value has a direct effect on competitive value. The latter is obtained through the contribution of IT to firm performance, innovation and the protection of resources. IT can contribute to two different aspects of firm performance: market performance, measured by for example stock market reactions and Tobin's q, and accounting performance, which can be measured by return on sales, return on assets, return on investment, etc. [54].

We mentioned that Schryen [54] distinguishes between tangible and intangible value. Both types of value can be found in internal as well as in external value. Productivity gains is an example of internal tangible value, while market

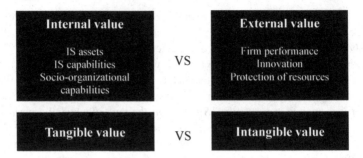

Fig. 5.2 Types of business value from IT-related investments [54]

performance can be categorized as external tangible value. The IS management capabilities are internal intangible value. An example of external intangible value is the protection of resources. The main challenge lies in measuring intangible value. As monitoring and evaluating value delivery requires value to be measured, it is crucial to cope with this challenge. Therefore, Schryen [54] proposes two strategies. Sometimes it might be too difficult to attribute a numerical value to intangible value types. Then, one could 'measure' value by comparing the current state with the former states or comparing the organization's position to the position of competitors, thereby creating some kind of ranking. As such, instead of attributing a numerical value to for example IS management capabilities, an organization could determine whether or not those capabilities have improved over the last year. An alternative strategy would be the use of perceptual measures, i.e. how did the IS management capabilities change according to an individual manager?

In conclusion, boards should ensure business value optimization from IT-related investments. In order to do so, they should carefully consider different types of value and how these types of value can be measured (summarized in Fig. 5.2).

5.4   Ensured Risk Optimization (EDM03)

Today, every enterprise is exploring either traditional or emerging technologies to create and protect business value. Nonetheless, such an expedition has exposed most of the technology dependent firms with significant challenges of operational IT risk, cyber security, and data privacy and compliance issues. In this view, COBIT 2019's risk optimization objective provides suitable guidance to the board of directors on IT-related risks.

As described in COBIT 2019, the purpose of 'Ensure risk optimization' as a governance objective is three-fold. First, the objective essentially tries to examine and understand the risk seeking and risk tolerance of the enterprise in the context of IT. Second, the enterprise should clearly articulate and communicate the aggregated risk profile, status of risk, management actions through appropriate level of governance and management within the enterprise. Third, it is about the board's responsibility to monitor and evaluate the risk management, so that any failure related to compliance can be minimized. To envision the 'ensure risk optimization' governance objective, COBIT 2019 provides three governance practices. The first practice guides on how the enterprise should persistently examine and evaluate the effect of risk on the current and future use of IT in the enterprise. This practice actually assesses whether all the risks associated with IT which can be affecting enterprise value are identified and whether the enterprise possesses the appropriate risk appetite to manage them. The second governance practice recommended for this objective is about how the board members should direct so as to establish risk management practices (1) to ensure that the enterprise has suitable management practices for the risk arising from IT, and (2) actual IT risk does not exceed the board's risk appetite. In the third governance practice, the board is accountable for monitoring the key goals and metrics of the risk management processes as well as determining possible mitigation measures in case of problems or deviations on the established goals and metrics.

IT failures in the past have shown a significant value destruction for enterprises. As a result, *risk optimization* is by far one of the most critical governance objectives for the board of directors. For example, a major cyber breach at Target Corp in 2013 left the enterprise with significant financial losses, and resulted into severe implications for the board of directors [55, 56]. Especially, since more than a decade, IT risk management has become one of the key topics on the board agenda. While COBIT 2019 outlines optimal governance practices to mitigate IT risk, there are some complementary approaches to classify IT risk. A Director's Dashboard for IT Risk Governance proposed by Parent and Reich [57] classifies IT risks into IT Competence Risk, Infrastructure Risk, IT Project Risk, Business Continuity Risk, and Information Risk. Table 5.1 summarizes what key questions the board of directors needs to address for each type of IT risk.

We can draw two conclusions from Table 5.1. First, IT risk can be classified into different risk profiles. Especially, this classification provides several types of IT risks that can be considered important for the board of directors, and should be put on the board agenda for the governance of IT risk. Next, we can observe that COBIT 2019 provides a comprehensive set of governance practices to evaluate, direct, and monitor each of the IT risks. In sum, COBIT 2019 systematically addresses the risk identification, management, and evaluation related to IT, and therefore the risk optimization governance objective can be instrumental in guiding the board of directors on IT risk.

5.5 Ensured Resource Optimization (EDM04)

The optimization of business and IT-related resources is categorized as a governance objective as well. COBIT 2019 claims that the board is accountable to "*ensure that adequate and sufficient business and IT-related resources (people,*

Table 5.1 IT risk classification and mapping to COBIT 2019 [50, 57]

IT risk	Key questions for the board of directors	Mapping to COBIT 2019
IT competence risk	1. Has the Board committed to an ongoing training program with respect to information technology? 2. Has the Board recruited and appointed a Lead Director for information technology?	COBIT 2019 refers to e-Competence Framework (e-CF)—A common European Framework for ICT Professionals in all industry sectors—Part 1: Framework, 2016 and Skills Framework for the Information Age V6, 2015 to develop the IT competence including board members
Infrastructure risk	1. Does the Board have a thorough (rank-ordered) understanding of the IT infrastructure risks in the organization (based on discussions with the CIO and/or audit committee)? 2. Does the organization regularly engage outside agencies to test its security systems and to conduct security audits?	In COBIT 2019 infrastructure related risk is explicitly outlined more within the management objectives than the governance objectives (e.g. APO12 Managed risk, APO13 Managed security, APO14 Managed data)
IT project risk	1. Has the organization demonstrated a high rate of success with IT-enabled change projects within the last 3 years? 2. Has the organization developed competence in project management (e.g., Project Office, certification of project managers)?	In COBIT 2019, 'Managed Projects' is a separate management objective to address project management topics
Business continuity risk	1. Does a current Business Continuity Plan (BCP) exist that includes all IT-related assets (e.g., systems, documentation, information, and technology)? 2. Is this BCP tested periodically (e.g., an IT disaster is initiated and resolved)?	The risk optimization governance objective clearly incorporates this risk and specifies the enterprise goal of business service continuity and availability (EG06) to address this risk
Information risk	1. Does an officer of the company sign-off regarding compliance with explicit information privacy and security policies (that conform to laws and/or regulations)? 2. Does the organization have a Privacy Officer—a senior manager responsible for developing and testing policies—and sufficient authority to enforce them?	COBIT 5 already recognizes information as a key enabler for the enterprise governance of IT. COBIT 2019 acknowledges ISF, The Standard of Good Practice for Information Security 2016, and incorporates information risk topics within the risk optimization governance objective

process and technology) are available to support enterprise objectives effectively and, at optimal cost". Such resource optimization is crucial to deliver programs on time, on budget and meeting requirements and quality standards, which in turn supports the maintenance of a portfolio of competitive products and services, the optimization of the internal business process functionality and managed digital transformation programs.

The COBIT 2019 framework claims that a first step towards resource optimization is evaluating resource management. An organization should continually evaluate its current and future need for business and IT resources and its options to obtain such resources. Allocation and management principles to optimally support resource management should be subject to continuous evaluation as well. Next, the adoption of these resource management principles should be safeguarded by assigning responsibilities, communicating resource management strategies, defining key goals and metrics, etc. Lastly, these goals and metrics should be continuously monitored. It is essential to adequately cope with any resource-related problems, by making plans on how to identify, track and report those problems.

In order to ensure optimal resource management, the board should first take a look at its own resources, i.e. the board members. Theories such as the resource based view of the firm and the resource dependence theory indicate that on the one hand, board members themselves could be valuable resources for the firm in terms of IT governance [4, 12, 58] and on the other hand, board members can play a vital role in obtaining relevant resources [55, 59].

Indeed, the IT expertise of directors is mentioned by many academic researchers as a crucial element of the board's involvement in governing IT [20, 60, 61]. It is the board's task to monitor management. In order to adequately perform this task, IT expertise among board members is indispensable. That is, monitoring management entails determining whether they have established IT governance procedures, such as policies to ensure IT security and succession plans for key personnel, and evaluating whether these procedures are appropriate [13]. Evaluating this appropriateness requires IT-related competencies among board members [13, 20, 55]. Another board responsibility is IT-related strategic decision making. The IT expertise of board members is important for supporting strategic IT-related initiatives, as it can be considered to be a cognitive bias that influences strategic decisions. Similarly, a lack of such expertise might inhibit innovation [58].

I think it is important that you make an evaluation of the competences and the complementarity of your board because you can only discuss ICT at board level when you have enough, what I would call, IT savviness at board level.

—Non-executive board member

We should distinguish between independent and dependent directors in this discussion, as the value of their IT expertise slightly differs. Independent directors with IT expertise enable the board to provide advice to management, to facilitate access to external IT parties, to attract qualified IT management and to advocate for more IT budgets. Internal directors with IT expertise are important to make sure that the board understands the business costs of IT risks, enable the swift allocation of resources and support priority setting to adjust IT weaknesses [55].

In order to gain a better understanding of the IT competencies needed at the level of the board to adequately perform their IT oversight role, Valentine and Stewart [20, 60] created a set of director competencies. They suggest three main competencies, for which they provide detailed descriptions.

The first board competency is described as *"direct and govern technology-enabled strategy and planning to maximize the advantages of technology and enhance performance at all levels of the organization"*. According to Valentine and Stewart [20, 60], this means that board members should possess knowledge about current and new technologies, how these can provide opportunities to support business strategy and how these are used in the external environment. Furthermore, the board should be able to evaluate the organization's dependence on IT and how this dependence might evolve in the future. In terms of the board's monitoring role, board members should possess the right expertise to oversee the governance of IT on the management level, ensure IT compliance with laws and regulations and monitor to what extent IT supports the business strategy [20].

"Lead and govern business technology investment and risk" is a second crucial board competency. It entails the ability to take on a leadership role in leading a digital-savvy culture. Moreover, directors should be able to evaluate IT-related risks. Understanding how data and information can be relevant to the organization's needs and how technology can support stakeholder engagement is another element of this second competence. In order to adequately govern business technology investment, the board should be able to oversee IT governance on the management level, specifically with regard to the entire IT-related project life cycle. Governing business technology investment also requires board members to understand what to measure in order to track technology performance [20].

A last IT governance board competency is *"direct and govern technology-enabled innovation and value creation"*. Therefore, the board should understand how to obtain business value from IT-related investments, also in terms of the organization's competitive position and risks. Moreover, board members should understand what their role is in the governance of IT-related projects. Lastly, the board should possess basic knowledge on the costs, benefits and implications of different types of technologies and IT-related services, such as mobile technologies and outsourcing [20].

We can conclude that boards of directors should ensure the optimization of business and IT-related resources, starting with their own competencies. We provided an overview and detailed description of three IT governance competencies for board members, based on Valentine and Stewart [20, 60] (Fig. 5.3). In this discussion, it is important to note that boards should understand how management should handle technology, but they should not be aware of all technology details [60].

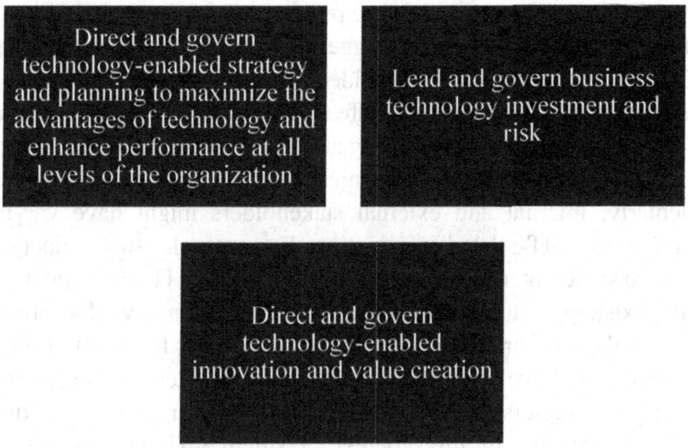

Fig. 5.3 Overview IT governance competencies for board members [20, 60]

5.6   Ensured Stakeholder Engagement (EDM05)

Enterprise governance of IT (EGIT) is recognized as a subset of corporate governance, and reflects most of its fundamental dimensions such as performance
measurement, policy and strategic planning, risk management, and ensuring
stakeholder transparency. In the context of EGIT, the term stakeholder transparency
can be twofold. That is, stakeholder transparency can encompass the interest of
internal as well as external stakeholders of an enterprise. The internal stakeholders
can include different levels of management within the enterprise, while external
stakeholder constitute shareholders, customers, regulatory institutions etc.
Acknowledging that information related to IT has value implications for most of the
internal and external stakeholders, providing timely and effective IT-related information is the responsibility of the board of directors. COBIT 2019 provides a robust
governance objective to ensure stakeholder transparency. The goal of this objective
is to first enhance the quality of IT management information, which has a direct
influence on the quality of financial and management information of the enterprise.
In other words, digital assets of the firm retrieve, store, and process management
and financial information of the enterprise, and therefore performance and con-
formance of IT is critical for the stakeholders. As a result, the board of directors
needs to improve reporting on EGIT to get support of stakeholders on the IT
strategy and roadmap. This can be achieved through effective and timely reporting
on the topic of IT.

   With 'ensure stakeholder engagement' as a governance objective, COBIT 2019
provides a set of governance practices that can be implemented to ensure stakeholder transparency. First, the objective warrants evaluating stakeholder engagement and reporting requirements. Especially, the board of directors should

constantly examine the current and future requirements for stakeholder engagement and reporting. Second, the objective suggests establishing a communication strategy for external and internal stakeholders. Lastly, the board should monitor stakeholder engagement levels and the effectiveness of stakeholder communication. While the board of directors acknowledges that communication on IT topics is of high importance, developing a communication strategy is always a challenging task. Particularly, internal and external stakeholders might have varying needs regarding the type of IT-related information. For example, shareholders might be interested in how the enterprise is doing on its previous IT investments; whereas, potential and existing customers might be eager to hear on new IT-enabled product or services that the enterprise will be offering in the near future. Both internal and external stakeholders have a significant impact on the enterprise's economic value, and the board of directors needs a suitable disclosure framework to disseminate relevant IT information. In this context, a suitable IT governance disclosure framework proposed by Joshi et al. [32] can provide a starting template for board members, which can supplement the governance objective of ensuring stakeholder transparency. As such, this disclosure framework was already mentioned as a tool to support task 3 "report" of our roadmap towards governing digital transformation. The following section briefly discusses the link between the disclosure framework and the COBIT 2019 guidelines.

The disclosure framework consists of four broad categories of IT governance (Table 5.2). The first category focuses on disclosure related to IT strategic alignment (ITSA). For example, an enterprise whose board or executive management appointed a CIO or equivalent on the board is likely to inform their stakeholders of such provisions. In this way, the enterprise can timely inform about an IT update at the board level. The second category (C2) relates to an enterprise's disclosure about value delivery on IT topics (ITVD). In this category, an enterprise can communicate about new IT projects, or status of the ongoing projects. The third category (C3), is about informing stakeholders on the topics of IT risk management issues (ITRM). The board of directors can provide disclosure on existing IT security issues, IT risk assessments, and risk mitigation efforts. In the final category, the enterprise can communicate on IT performance measurement (C4). This category can provide very valuable information to the external stakeholders on the range of economic parameters relevant for IT. For example, an enterprise can share information on IT expenditure, e.g. budget allocation for new IT projects. A closer look at all the disclosure categories reveals that the COBIT 2019 EDM governance objectives are well-integrated into the disclosure framework (see mapping column in Table 5.2), which makes it a suitable instrument for the board of directors to enhance stakeholder transparency.

In this section, we can conclude that the 'ensure stakeholder engagement' is a key governance objective to improve stakeholder involvement in the enterprise. The objective clearly encompasses the other four governance objectives as a source on which engagement can be established. That is, an enterprise can communicate on the topic of governance framework and maintenance, benefits delivery, risk optimization, and resource optimization to ensure stakeholder involvement in the

Table 5.2 IT governance disclosure framework [32]

Items	Mapping on COBIT 2019
Panel A: (C1) IT Strategic Alignment (ITSA)	
IT expert on the board	The ITSA category maps well with the EDM01— ensured governance framework setting and maintenance, as it systematically covers the governance practices for EDM01
IT expert with experience on the board	
A CIO or an equivalent position in the firm	
IT committee	
IT Risk is part of audit committee or risk committee	
IT is part of audit committee	
IT steering committee	
IT planning committee	
Technology committee	
IT committee at an executive level	
A CIO or an equivalent is on the board	
Panel B: (C2) IT Value Delivery (ITVD)	
IT governance framework/standard: ITIL/COBIT/ISO etc.	The ITVD disclosure category essentially captures the objective and alignment goals of EDM02— ensured benefits delivery, and is also relevant to EDM01—ensured governance framework setting and maintenance
IT as an issue in the board meeting	
Suggestion/decision/advise by the board on IT	
Special report/section on IT/IT projects in annual report	
IT mentioned as a strategic business issue	
IT projected as strength	
IT projected as opportunity	
Project updates or comments	
IT is explicitly mentioned for achieving specific business objectives	
Comments/Updates on IT performance	
IT training	
Green IT	
Direction and status about IT outsourcing and in-sourcing	
Panel C: (C3) IT Risk Management (ITRM)	
IT is referred under operational risk	The ITRM category mainly maps onto EDM03— Ensured risk optimization governance objective
Special IT risk management program	
Use of IT for regulation and compliance	

(continued)

Table 5.2 (continued)

Items	Mapping on COBIT 2019
IT/Electronic Data Processing (EDP) audit	
Information and security policy/plan (IT security)	
The role of IT in accounting and the reporting standards (IAS)	
Operations continuity plan	
Panel D: (C4) IT Performance Measurement (ITPM)	
Explicit information on IT expenditure	The ITPM category covers the objective of EDM02 —Ensured Benefits Delivery and EDM04—Ensured Resource Optimization
IT budget	
IT hardware cost	
IT software cost	
Explicit IT manpower cost is mentioned	
IT expenses are mentioned under administrative cost	
IT related assets are mentioned under intangible assets	
Direct cost on IT is mentioned in currency or percentage	

enterprise. In addition, the enterprise can supplement such an objective with the support of the existing IT governance disclosure framework.

5.7 Conclusion

In this chapter, we showed that the widely-used COBIT 2019 framework also recognizes the responsibilities of the board of directors with regard to IT governance. The COBIT 2019 guidelines allowed us to elaborate on certain parts of the previously proposed roadmap.

COBIT 2019 suggests five governance objectives for which the board of directors is accountable. In the previous chapters these governance objectives were discussed as described by the framework and more specific guidance was introduced from academic research. The first objective states that the board should ensure that a governance arrangement or framework is put in place and effectively maintained. More specific guidance was provided for example by providing some examples of principles for IT governance used in real-life organizations to inspire board members on the type of principles that could be included.

The second governance objective specifically focusses on benefits delivery, i.e. ensuring the optimization of business value from IT-related investments. We elaborated on the types of business value that can be produced by IT. That is, boards should both consider internal value, such as productivity gains, and external value in the form of firm performance but also innovation and protection of resources. Moreover, value can be tangible as well as intangible. The main challenge lies in measuring this intangible value. We discussed some strategies to cope with this challenge.

Third, risks related to IT can no longer be ignored at board level. A classification of IT risk was presented, which categorizes IT risks into IT Competence Risk, Infrastructure Risk, IT Project Risk, Business Continuity Risk, and Information Risk. We have shown how these types of risk are addressed in the COBIT 2019 framework.

Fourth, the board should ensure the optimization of business as well as IT-related resources in order to support the business strategy at an optimal cost. We argue that the board should first consider its own resources, i.e. the board members. An overview of three key IT governance director competencies was provided.

The last governance objective relates to the topic of stakeholder transparency. More specifically, the board should report in an effective and timely manner on IT-related topics. An instrumental disclosure framework was introduced that provides the board with some suggestions on which topics to report on in the context of external disclosure.

References

1. OECD *G20/OECD Principles of Corporate Governance*. 2015.
2. Valentine, E. and G. Stewart. 2015. Enterprise business technology governance: Three Competencies to Build Board Digital Leadership Capability. In *48th Hawaii International Conference on System Sciences*. 2015. IEEE.
3. Coertze, J. and R. von Solms. 2014. The board and CIO: The IT alignment challenge. In *47th Hawaii International Conference on System Sciences*. IEEE.
4. Valentine, E., and G. Stewart. 2013. The emerging role of the Board of Directors in enterprise business technology governance. *International Journal of Disclosure and Governance* 10 (4): 346–362.
5. Andriole, S., 2009. *Boards of Directors and Technology Governance: The Surprising State of the Practice*. Communications of the Association for Information Systems.
6. Bart, C. and O. Turel. 2010. *IT and the Board of Directors: An Empirical Investigation into the "Governance Questions" Canadian Board Members Ask about IT*.
7. Trautman, L., and K. Altenbaumer-Price. 2011. The board's responsibility for information technology governance. *The John Marshall Journal of Computer and Information Law* 28 (3): 313–341.
8. Butler, R., and M.J. Butler. 2010. Beyong King III: Assigning accountability for IT governance in South African enterprises. *South African Journal of Business Management* 41 (3): 33–45.
9. Parent, M. and B.H. Reich. 2009. Governing information technology risk. *California Management Review*. 51 (3): 134–+.
10. Raghupathi, W. 2007. Corporate governance of IT: A framework for development. *Communications of the ACM* 50 (8): 94–99.
11. Healy, P., and K. Palepu. 2001. Information asymmetry, corporate disclosure, and the capital markets: A review of the empirical disclosure literature. *Journal of Accounting and Economics* 31: 405–440.
12. Turel, O., and C. Bart. 2014. Board-level IT governance and organizational performance. *European Journal of Information Systems* 23 (2): 223–239.
13. Trites, G. 2004. Director responsibility for IT governance. *International Journal of Accounting Information Systems* 5 (2): 89–99.
14. O'Donnell, E. 2004. Discussion of director responsibility for IT governance: a perspective on strategy. *International Journal of Accounting Information Systems* 5 (2): 101–104.
15. Weill, P. and J.W. Ross. 2004. *IT governance: How top performers manage IT decision rights for superior results*. 2004: Harvard Business Press.

© Springer Nature Switzerland AG 2020

S. De Haes et al., *Governing Digital Transformation*, Management for Professionals,
https://doi.org/10.1007/978-3-030-30267-2

16. Venkatraman, N., J.C. Henderson, and S. Oldach. 1993. Continuous strategic alignment: Exploiting information technology capabilities for competitive success. *European Management Journal* 11 (2): 139–149.
17. Butler, R., and M.J. Butler. 2010. Beyond King III: Assigning accountability for IT governance in South African enterprises. *South African Journal of Business Management* 41 (3): 33–45.
18. IT Governance Institute (ITGI). 2003. *Board Briefing on IT Governance, 2nd Edition.*
19. Posthumus, S., R. von Solms, and M. King. 2010. The board and IT governance: The what, who and how. *South African Journal of Business Management* 41 (3): 23–32.
20. Valentine, E. and G. Stewart. 2015. Enterprise business technology governance: Three competencies to build board digital leadership capability. In *2015 48th Hawaii International Conference on System Sciences*, T.X. Bui and R.H. Sprague, Editors. 2015. pp. 4513-4522.
21. Van Grembergen, W. and S. De Haes, *Enterprise governance of information technology: achieving strategic alignment and value.* 2009: Springer Science & Business Media.
22. Peterson, R. 2004. Crafting information technology governance. *Information systems management* 21 (4): 7–22.
23. Jewer, J., and K.N. McKay. 2012. Antecedents and consequences of board IT governance: institutional and strategic choice perspectives. *Journal of the Association for Information Systems* 13 (7): 581–617.
24. Nolan, R. and F.W. McFarlan. 2005. Information technology and the board of directors. *Harvard Business Review* 83(10): 96−+.
25. Kaplan, R.S., and D.P. Norton. 1993. Putting the balanced scorecard to work. *Harvard Business Review* 71 (5): 134–142.
26. Read, T.J. 2004. Discussion of director responsibility for IT governance. *International journal of accounting information systems* 5 (2): 105–107.
27. Bart, C., and O. Turel. 2010. IT and the board of directors: An empirical investigation into the "governance questions" Canadian board members ask about IT. *Journal of Information Systems* 24 (2): 147–172.
28. OECD, *G20/OECD Principles of Corporate Governance.* 2015.
29. Healy, P.M., and K.G. Palepu. 2001. Information asymmetry, corporate disclosure, and the capital markets: A review of the empirical disclosure literature. *Journal of Accounting & Economics* 31 (1–3): 405–440.
30. Higgs, J.L., et al. 2016. The relationship between board-level technology committees and reported security breaches. *Journal of Information Systems* 30 (3): 79–98.
31. Gordon, L.A., M.P. Loeb, and T. Sohail. 2010. *Market value of voluntary disclosures concerning information security.* MIS quarterly, 567–594.
32. Joshi, A., L. Bollen, and H. Hassink. 2013. An empirical assessment of IT governance transparency: Evidence from commercial banking. *Information Systems Management* 30 (2): 116–136.
33. Zhu, K., K.L. Kraemer, and J. Dedrick. 2004. Information technology payoff in e-business environments: An international perspective on value creation of e-business in the financial services industry. *Journal of management information systems* 21 (1): 17–54.
34. Chatterjee, D., V.J. Richardson, and R.W. Zmud. 2001. *Examining the shareholder wealth effects of announcements of newly created CIO positions.* Mis Quarterly: 43–70.
35. Dehning, B., V.J. Richardson, and R.W. Zmud. 2003. *The value relevance of announcements of transformational information technology investments.* Mis Quarterly, 2003: 637–656.
36. Turel, O., P. Liu, and C. Bart. 2017. Board-Level Information Technology Governance Effects on Organizational Performance: the Roles of Strategic Alignment and Authoritarian Governance Style. *Information Systems Management* 34 (2): 117–136.
37. Eisenhardt, K.M. 1989. Agency theory: An assessment and review. *Academy of management review* 14 (1): 57–74.
38. Posthumus, S. and R. von Solms. 2008. *Agency theory: Can it be used to strengthen IT governance?* in *23rd IFIP International Information Security Conference.*

39. Donaldson, L., and J.H. Davis. 1991. Stewardship theory or agency theory: CEO governance and shareholder returns. *Australian Journal of management* 16 (1): 49–64.
40. Daily, C.M., D.R. Dalton, and A.A. Cannella. 2003. Corporate governance: Decades of dialogue and data. *Academy of management review* 28 (3): 371–382.
41. Huse, M. 2005. Accountability and creating accountability: A framework for exploring behavioural perspectives of corporate governance. *British Journal of Management* 16 (s1): S65–S79.
42. Johnson, J.L., C.M. Daily, and A.E. Ellstrand. 1996. Boards of directors: A review and research agenda. *Journal of management* 22 (3): 409–438.
43. Pfeffer, J.. 1972. Size and composition of corporate boards of directors: The organization and its environment. *Administrative Science Quarterly*: 218–228.
44. Kuruzovich, J., G. Bassellier, and V. Sambamurthy. 2012. IT governance processes and IT alignment: Viewpoints from the board of directors. In *45th Hawaii International Conference on System Science (HICSS)*. 2012. IEEE.
45. Coertze, J. and R. von Solms. 2014. *The Board and CIO: The IT Alignment Challenge*. In *2014 47th Hawaii International Conference on System Sciences*: 4426–4435.
46. De Haes, S. and W. Van Grembergen, *Enterprise governance of information technology*. 2015: Springer.
47. De Haes, S., W. Van Grembergen, and R.S. Debreceny. 2013. COBIT 5 and enterprise governance of information technology: Building blocks and research opportunities. *Journal of Information Systems* 27 (1): 307–324.
48. Bharadwaj, A., et al. 2013. Digital business strategy: toward a next generation of insights. *MIS Quarterly*: 471–482.
49. Tiwana, A., and S.K. Kim. 2015. Discriminating IT governance. *Information Systems Research* 26 (4): 656–674.
50. ISACA, *COBIT 2019 Framework: Introduction & Methodology*. 2018.
51. ISO/IEC, *ISO/IEC Standard 38500: Information technology—Governance of IT for the organization*. 2015.
52. Peterson, R.R. 2004. Integration strategies and tactics for information technology governance. In *Strategies for information technology governance*. Igi Global: 37–80.
53. ISACA, *COBIT 5: A Business Framework for the Governance and Management of Enterprise IT*. 2012.
54. Schryen, G. 2013. Revisiting IS business value research: what we already know, what we still need to know, and how we can get there. *European Journal of Information Systems* 22 (2): 139–169.
55. Benaroch, M., and A. Chernobai. 2017. Operational IT failures, IT value-destruction, and board-level IT governance changes. *MIS quarterly* 41 (3): 729–762.
56. Srinivasan, S., L. Paine, and N. Goyal, *Cyber Breach at Target*. 2016, Boston MA: Business Case, Harvard Buiness School Publishing
57. Parent, M., and B.H. Reich. 2009. Governing information technology risk. *California Management Review* 51 (3): 134–152.
58. Héroux, S., and A. Fortin. 2018. The moderating role of IT-business alignment in the relationship between IT governance, IT competence, and innovation. *Information Systems Management* 35 (2): 98–123.
59. Yayla, A.A., and Q. Hu. 2014. The effect of Board of directors' IT awareness on CIO compensation and firm performance. *Decision Sciences* 45 (3): 401–436.
60. Valentine, E. and G. Stewart. 2013. Director competencies for effective enterprise technology governance. In *Proceedings of the 24th Australasian Conference on Information Systems (ACIS 2013)*.
61. Mohamad, S., et al. 2014. Developing a model to evaluate the information technology competence of boards of directors. *Corporate Ownership & Control* 12 (1): 12.

Printed in the United States
By Bookmasters